The Customs of Catalonia

between

Lords and Vassals

BY THE BARCELONA CANON, PERE ALBERT:
A PRACTICAL GUIDE TO CASTLE FEUDALISM
IN MEDIEVAL SPAIN

Medieval and Renaissance Texts and Studies

Volume 2 4 3

Mediterranean Studies Monographs and Texts

Volume 1

Guy Mermier, General Editor

The Customs of Catalonia
between
Lords and Vassals

BY THE BARCELONA CANON, PERE ALBERT:
A PRACTICAL GUIDE TO CASTLE FEUDALISM
IN MEDIEVAL SPAIN

translation and commentary by
Donald J. Kagay

Arizona Center for Medieval and Renaissance Studies
Tempe, Arizona
2002

The publication of this volume has been greatly assisted by a grant from the Program for Cultural Cooperation between Spain's Ministry of Education, Culture and Sports and United States Universities.

Dust jacket image: Capital S: Prosecuting attorney taking witness testimony. James III, King of Majorca, *Leges Palatinae* (facsimile), ed. Jose J. Olaneta (Bloomington, IN, 1994), fol. 40v.

Library of Congress Cataloging-in-Publication Data
Albert, Pere, 13th cent.
   [Commemorationes. English]
   The customs of Catalonia between lords and vassals / by the Barcelona canon, Pere Albert ; a practical guide to castle feudalism in medieval Spain ; translation and commentary by Donald J. Kagay.
   p. cm. — (Medieval & Renaissance Texts & Studies ; v. 243)
   Includes bibliographical references and index.
   ISBN 0-86698-285-X (alk. paper)
   1. Feudal law — Spain — Catalonia — History — To 1500. I. Kagay, Donald J. II. Title. III. Medieval & Renaissance Texts & Studies (Series) ; v. 243.
KKT220.213.A2 2002
340.5'5 —dc21   2002018434

This book is made to last.
It is set in Bembo,
smythe-sewn and printed on acid-free paper
to library specifications.

Contents

Acknowledgments

I would like to thank Dr. Robert E. Bjork and Ms. Laura Gross of the Arizona Center for Medieval and Renaissance Studies as well as the two readers of this work and its copy editor whose criticisms and suggestions have made me consider questions I had not confronted in the various versions of either the introduction or the translation. I must also thank my friends and colleagues, Dr. Paul Chevedden, Dr. Theresa Vann, and Dr. Andrew Villalon, whose openhanded advice and encouragement about this project have never flagged. Because of their creative input, this is a much better book.

I would also like to extend my heartfelt thanks to President Portia Holmes Shields as well as Dean Michael Rogers of the Graduate School of Albany State University for their invaluable support of the research for this volume.

Abbreviations

ACA	Arxiu de la Corona d'Aragó, Barcelona
ACB	Arxiu Capitular de Barcelona
AEM	*Anuario de Estudios Medievales*
AHDE	*Anuario de Historia del Derecho Español*
AHR	*American Historical Review*
BRABLB	*Boletín de la Real Academia de Buenas Letras de Barcelona*
BRAH	*Boletin de la Real Academia de Historia*
CAVC	*Colección de los cortes de los antiguos reinos de Aragón y de Valencia y el principado de Cataluña*
CDACA	*Colección inéditos del Archivo General de la Corona de Aragón*
CHCA	*Congrés d'Història de la Corona d'Aragó* [congress number indicated in Roman numerals]
CSCV	*Cartulario de Sant Cugat del Vallès*
CSJP	*Cronica de San Juan de la Peña*
DB	*Diccionari biogràfic*
DJ	*Documentos de Jaime I*
DMA	*Dictionary of the Middle Ages*
DS	*Documenta Selecta*
fol.; fols.	folio; folios

ABBREVIATIONS

GCB	*Gesta Comitium Barchinonensis*
LF	*Llibre dels Feyts*
LFM	*Liber Feudorum Maior*
Marca	*Marca Hispanica*
MRAH	*Memorias de la Real Academia de la Historia*
MS.; MSS.	manuscript, manuscripts
Notule	The Register *"Notule Communium 14"* of the Diocese of Barcelona
R.	Register
RABM	*Revista de los Archivos, Bibliotecas y Museos*

Introduction

The Significance of Pere Albert's Customs of Catalonia: A Pale Light in a Heavy Fog

Few terms have caused wider or more persistent misunderstanding than those associated with feudal tenure and allegiance. Largely the same body of northern European evidence has provided the raw material for drastically divergent interpretations of the role of feudal relations within medieval society. One school, the "deconstructionist," denies the viability of "feudalism" as a foundation of historical truth, but rather asserts that it is all but impossible to talk of general feudal practice at any period of the Middle Ages. According to one of the founders of this view, Elizabeth Brown, feudalism was an anachronistic abstraction which owed its existence, not to any real evidence, but rather to the efforts of early modern lawyers and historians who manufactured a "feudal system" where there had been none. To Brown and Susan Reynolds, the most recent scholar to build on her views,[1] misconceptions about the regime of lords and vassals could not arise from the contemporary documentation because such evidence was so scattered and unclear that it could support no intellectual system whatsoever. Instead, they assert, the modern world got feudalism wrong, because of a class of royal advocates and legists of the thirteenth and fourteenth centuries, as well as their counterparts in the *ancien régime*, who all attempted to make the scattered relics of feudal relations fit into a system which was topped by the monarch himself. Thus was born the "feudal pyramid," a model which the "deconstructionists" claim was invented out of thin air and then accepted uncritically by such early modern legal and political theorists as Sir Edward Coke, François Hotman, Sir Thomas Craig,

---

[1] Elizabeth A. R. Brown, "The Tyranny of a Construct: Feudalism and the Historians of Medieval Europe," *AHR* 79 (1974): 1063–89; Susan Reynolds, *Fiefs and Vassals: The Medieval Evidence Reinterpreted* (Oxford, 1994), 775–86.

ix

and Sir Henry Spelman.[2] Their views comprised a learned orthodoxy which dominated the general discussions of medieval institutions for the last three centuries. The scholarly acceptance of this "construct" is what Brown and Reynolds have set out to negate. In the process, the very term "feudalism" has been scrupulously avoided in monograph and textbook alike.[3]

Another interpretation of the world of feudal relations, the "social" school, looks to the era of societal disintegration accompanying the barbarian invasions as the seed-time for the formation and development of such typically feudal elements as the castle and the fief, as well as social relationships which made them viable. The acculturative model, the work of scholars such as Abilio Barbero, Marcelo Vigil, Pierre Bonnassie, Guy Bois, and Thomas F. Glick, is especially well suited to the Iberian Peninsula and other regions of the southern Mediterranean.[4] With the fluid interaction in these areas among social groups, even those divided by ethnic, linguistic, and religious factors, feudal relations become one of a number of societal elements, which, like many forms of technology, were adapted, exchanged, and altered within a multi-cultural hot house of sorts, a social atmosphere referred to by Américo Castro as "coexistence" or *convivencia*.[5]

As is so often the case, truth is often elastic enough to support any number of positions if they are couched in a skillful enough way. The resultant welter of scholarly claim and counterclaim is, to use Marc Bloch's phrase, a classic "paper

---

[2] For the work of common-law authorities, see J. G. A. Pocock, *The Ancient Constitution and the Feudal Law: A Study of English Historical Thought in the Seventeenth Century* (Cambridge, 1957; repr. New York, 1967; new ed. with additions Cambridge, 1987), 70–123.

[3] For examples of the "deconstructionist" influence on current historiography, see James A. Brundage, *Medieval Canon Law* (London, 1995), 30–31; Jean-Pierre Poly and Eric Bournazel, *The Feudal Transformation, 900–1200*, trans. Caroline Higgitt (New York, 1991), 351–57.

[4] Abilio Barbero and Marcelo Vigil, *La formación del feudalismo en la península ibérica* (Barcelona, 1978; repr. Barcelona, 1986); Pierre Bonnassie, *From Slavery to Feudalism in South-Western Europe*, trans. Jean Birrell (Cambridge, 1991); Guy Bois, *The Transformation of the Year One Thousand* (Manchester, 1992); Thomas F. Glick, *From Muslim Fortress to Christian Castle: Social and Cultural Change in Medieval Spain* (Manchester, 1995).

[5] Américo Castro, *The Spaniards: An Introduction to Their History*, trans. Willard F. King and Selma Margaretten (Berkeley, 1971), 584; Vivian Mann, Thomas F. Glick, and Jerrilynn D. Dodds, eds., *Convivencia: Jews, Muslim, and Christians in Medieval Spain* (New York, 1992), 1–6; Joseph F. O'Callaghan, *A History of Medieval Spain* (Ithaca, NY, 1975), 17–24.

war."[6] Thus between the poles of an indigenous, largely uninterpretable body of feudal evidence and the model of social interaction across political, religious, and linguistic frontiers, there stands the subject of this work: the *Customs of Catalonia* of the thirteenth-century Barcelona canon Pere Albert. As a handbook for the adjudication of feudal differences, Pere Albert's work is neither "deconstructionist" nor "social," but legal in an intensely practical way. This is clearly reflected in the work's subtitle, the *Commemorationes*, a term related to the Latin words *commemoratorium* and *memoria*, which were generally used to mean a report or memorandum. Such "white papers" could be used in a number of situations by lawyers or royal officials attempting to bolster their legal position by gathering pertinent documents, arranging them in a logical order, and appending relevant commentary when necessary. These documents were important in administrative terms, as well as in the arena of civil or criminal law.[7] Thus while its significance may be overlooked by the two above-discussed views, the *Customs of Catalonia*'s relative lack of scholastic or Romanist guile is what recommends it. Rather than encapsulating a "system," Pere Albert's book tries to provide a simplified adjudicative guide to the overgrown garden of feudal relations in his day.

Notwithstanding what modern historiography has viewed as its shortcomings, Pere Albert's work must be considered invaluable because of, and not despite, its simple nature. Like a number of continental and Iberian works of the thirteenth and fourteenth centuries, the *Customs of Catalonia* was not a work of jurisprudential theory. It had little connection to such treatises of twelfth-century feudal law as the *Constitutio* of Conrad II or the *Libri Feudorum*, which had attempted to mold individual statutes into a unified system of law similar to the *Code* of Justinian which had been rediscovered in Italy in the eleventh century.[8] The *Customs of Catalonia*, instead, had much more in common with such contemporaneous col-

---

[6] Marc Bloch, *Feudal Society*, trans. L. A. Manyon, 2 vols. (Chicago, 1961), 1:xx.

[7] Thomas N. Bisson, ed., *Fiscal Accounts of Catalonia under the Early Count-Kings (1151–1213)*, 2 vols. (Berkeley, 1984), 1:18; idem, *Tormented Voices: Power, Crisis, and Humanities in Rural Catalonia, 1140–1200* (Cambridge, MA, 1998), 3–5.

[8] Reynolds, *Fiefs and Vassals*, 216–17, 483–86; Harold J. Berman, *Law and Revolution: The Formation of the Western Legal Tradition* (Cambridge, MA, 1983), 310–11; Paul Vinogradoff, *Roman Law in Medieval Europe* (Oxford, 1929), 736; Charles Donahue, "Law, Civil" in *Dictionary of the Middle Ages* [hereafter *DMA*], ed. Joseph R. Strayer et al., 13 vols. (New York, 1982–1989), 7:418–25; John B. Freed, "Constitutio de Feudis," in *DMA*, 3:557–58; David Herlihy, ed., *The History of Feudalism* (New York, 1970), 107–9, doc. 22.

lections as the *Leges Henrici Primi*,[9] the *On the Laws and Customs of England* of Henry de Bracton,[10] the anonymous treatise entitled *Modus Tenendi Parlamenti*,[11] Philippe de Beaumanoir's *Coutumes de Beauvaisis*,[12] and the Catalan adjudicative handbook attributed by some to Pere Albert himself, the *Consuetudo Barcinonae*.[13] All of these works were composed by practicing attorneys for their own use or as handbooks for their fellows in the legal profession. The purpose of the *Customs of Catalonia*, then, was not to display dazzling legal erudition, but rather to provide a clear exposition of what Catalan feudal custom was and how disputes among lords, vassals, and other tenants were to be legally settled. The significance of Pere Albert's work is thus legal and institutional. A little over a century after its appearance, the *Customs of Catalonia*, along with the *Usatges of Barcelona* and the legislation of the Catalan parliament, the *Corts*, were accepted as a body of fundamental law for Catalonia.[14] In addition to its ultimate importance as statute, Pere Albert's work is crucial for understanding the emergent feudal norms of thirteenth-century Catalonia and emphasizes the need for a reassessment of such manuals throughout medieval Europe in order to better inform all the current schools of feudal research.

Jaume I (1213–1276): Conqueror and Lawgiver

The political and legal backdrop before which Pere Albert, as advocate, judge, and legal theorist, acted was the long and eventful reign of Jaume I "the Conqueror" (1213–1276). Effectively orphaned with the death of his father, Pere I (1196–1213), at the battle of Muret (13 September 1213), the young heir to Aragon and Catalonia spent his early years as the hostage of his father's arch-enemy, Simon de Montfort, or under the corrupt and self-seeking tutelage of two successive regency

---

[9] Berman, *Law and Revolution*, 74; Fredric L. Cheyette, "The Invention of the State," in *Essays on Medieval Civilization*, ed. Bede K. Lackner and Kenneth R. Philp (Austin, 1978), 158–59.

[10] Henry de Bracton, *On the Laws and Customs of England*, trans. Samuel E. Thorne, 4 vols. (Cambridge, MA, 1977), 3:xxx–xxxix.

[11] Ronald Butt, *A History of Parliament: The Middle Ages* (London, 1989), 218–19.

[12] Philippe de Beaumanoir, *The Coutumes de Beauvaisis*, trans. F. R. P. Akehurst (Philadelphia, 1992).

[13] Ferran Valls i Taberner, "Un articulat inèdit de *Consuetuds de Barcelona*," in idem, *Obras selectas*, 4 vols. (Madrid, 1954–1961), 2:142–47.

[14] José María Font Rius, ed., *Constitucions de Catalunya* (Barcelona, 1988).

councils.[15] Emerging from an adolescence marked by the actions of "evil men who oppress our lands in many ways,"[16] Jaume was able to obtain political dominance by an unflagging confidence in himself which he repeatedly tested by taking up the mantle of reconquest warrior and crusader against Islam, a profession he would practice from his early teens until he was almost seventy.[17] With little but this unshakeable belief in his own destiny, the young sovereign began probing the defenses of the neighboring Muslim states of Valencia and Majorca. Gaining the support of his clergy and barons, Jaume supervised a series of brilliant campaigns between 1229 and 1244, which led to the extension of his authority over much of *Sharq al-Andalus*, the easternmost provinces of Muslim Spain.[18] Dying on campaign at the age of sixty-eight in the summer of 1276, the Conqueror had devoted his later years to the defense of what he had conquered. In effect, all of his territorial gains seemed to have been at jeopardy with an invasion of Moroccan Muslims as well as the rebellions of his own Christian and Muslim subjects.[19]

---

[15] Lynn H. Nelson, trans., *The Chronicle of San Juan de la Peña: A Fourteenth-Century Official History of the Crown of Aragon* [hereafter *CSJP*] (Philadelphia, 1991), 61, chap. 35; Salvador Sanpere y Miquel, "Minoría de Jaime I," in *Congrés d'història de la corona d'Aragó, dedicat al rey En Jaume I i a la seva època* [hereafter I *CHCA*], 2 vols. (Barcelona, 1909–1913), 2:581–89; Ferran Soldevila, *Els primers temps de Jaume I* (Barcelona, 1968), 45–155; Charles Oman, *History of the Art of War during the Middle Ages, A.D. 378–1485*, 2 vols. (London, 1924), 1:453–61; J. R. Maddicott, *Simon de Montfort* (Cambridge, 1995), 4.

[16] Donald J. Kagay, "Royal Power in an Urban Setting: James I and the Towns of the Crown of Aragon," *Mediaevistik* 8 (1995): 127–36, esp. 131.

[17] Robert I. Burns, S.J, "The Spiritual Life of James the Conqueror: Portrait and Self-Portrait," in *Jaime I y su época* [hereafter X *CHCA*], 2 vols. (Zaragoza, 1976), Comunicaciones 1–2:333–35; Donald J. Kagay, "Structures of Baronial Dissent and Revolt under James I (1213–76)," *Mediaevistik* 1 (1988): 68–69.

[18] Micaela Danús, "Conquesta y repoblación de Mallorca: Notas sobre Nicoláu Bovet," X *CHCA*, Comunicaciones 1–2:41–64; Charles Julian Bishko, "The Spanish and Portuguese Reconquest," in *A History of the Crusades*, ed. Kenneth Setton et al., 6 vols. (Madison, WI, 1962–1975), 3:400–5; Alvaro Santamaría, "La expansión político-militar de la Corona de Aragón: Baleares," X *CHCA*, Ponencias, 91–109; Antonio Ubieto Arteta, "La reconquista de Valencia y Murcia," X *CHCA*, Ponencias, 147–66.

[19] *CSJP*, 66–68, chap. 35; Ferran Soldevila, *Pere el Gran*, 2 vols. (Barcelona, 1950–1962), 2:415–17, 420–23; *Llibre dels Fets del Rei en Jaume* [hereafter *LF*], ed. Jordi Bruguera, 2 vols. (Barcelona, 1991), 2:286–87, chaps. 565–66; Robert I. Burns, S.J. and Paul E. Chevedden, *Negotiating Cultures: Bilingual Surrender Treaties in Muslim-Christian Spain* (Leiden, 1999); eidem, " 'The Finest Castle in the World'," *History Today* 49 (11) (November, 1999): 10–17.

Along with an ambition for the expansion of domestic power and foreign conquest, Jaume's life was also defined by his role as legislator and protector of the law. As "sovereign lord" of Catalonia, Aragon, and all his newly-conquered lands, the king stood as the guarantor of the "common good" of his people.[20] He carried out this role through the customary exercise of his "jurisdiction," "dominion," and "authority."[21] Recognizing no political superior "in his own lands," Jaume nonetheless was bound by the law to carry out his duties, which were just as carefully defined by that same law. To earn his name as sovereign, Jaume, like his grandfather Alfons I (1163–1196), was obliged to "do good, right wrongs in punishing injuries, in quieting battles, in solidifying the peace, and in hearing cases."[22] In immediate terms, such high-minded ideals were translated into royal lawgiving and judgement.

Like his predecessors, Jaume seemed a bottomless source of individual privileges. When his largesse extended to corporate groups among his own corelig-

---

[20] On evolving political theory of "common good" in the Middle Ages, see M. S. Kempshall, *The Common Good in Late Medieval Political Thought* (Oxford, 1999); Joseph Canning, *A History of Medieval Political Thought, 300–1450* (London, 1996), 112–13, 138–30; Kenneth Pennington, *The Prince and the Law, 1200–1600: Sovereignty and Rights in Western Legal Tradition* (Berkeley, 1993), 235–36; D. E. Luscombe and G. R. Evans, "The Twelfth-Century Renaissance," in *The Cambridge History of Medieval Political Thought*, ed. J. H. Burns (Cambridge, 1988), 311; Anthony Black, *Political Thought in Europe, 1250–1450* (London, 1996), 24–26; idem, "The individual and society," in *Cambridge History*, 596–97.

[21] Gaines Post, *Studies in Medieval Legal Thought, Public Law and the State, 1100–1321* (Princeton, 1968), 112, 253–60; José Antonio Maravall, *Estudios de historia del pensamiento español*, 2 vols. (Madrid, 1983), 1:462–63; 2:150–51; Donald J. Kagay, "The King's Right Must be Preferred to the Lord's: Sovereignty and Suzerainty in the Treaties of Pere Albert," *Proceedings of the Tenth International Congress of Medieval Canon Law*, forthcoming; William E. Brynteson, "Roman Law and Legislation in the Middle Ages," *Speculum* 41 (1966): 420–37, esp. 420–24.

[22] *Colección de los cortes de los antiguos reinos de Aragón y de Valencia y el principado de Cataluña* [hereafter *CAVC*], ed. Fidel Fita y Colomé and Bienvenido Oliver y Estreller, 27 vols. (Madrid, 1896–1922), 1, pt. 1:55–56. For theory of kingship in thirteenth-century Iberia, see Maravall, *Estudios*, 1:95–98; Joseph F. O'Callaghan, "The Ideology of Government in the Reign of Alfonso X of Castile," *Exemplaria Hispanica* 1 (1991–1992): 8–10; idem, *The Learned King: The Reign of Alfonso X of Castile* (Philadelphia, 1993), 22–30; Thomas N. Bisson, "Prelude to Power: Kingship and Constitution in the Realms of Aragon, 1175–1250," in *The Worlds of Alfonso the Learned and James the Conqueror*, ed. Robert I. Burns, S.J. (Princeton, 1985), 23–40.

ionists as well as among the Jewish and Muslim communities under his rule, greater royal direction was needed and became manifest in the issuance of statutes (*fueros, furs*), which applied to all the territory and population of such groups.[23] In time, such prosaic and largely unconnected customs were amplified and restated by professional legists, becoming in the process the strains of foral law that stretched far from their municipal origins of Barcelona, Tortosa, or Teruel into many a town and hamlet of eastern Spain.[24] In addition to urban law, Jaume, like his predecessors in both Aragon and Catalonia from the eleventh century onward, made general enactments under the aegis of the peace and truce of God.[25] With the *pax et treuga*, the Catalan ruler found his legislative voice. In the process, the general protection of the peace came to form the "constitutional order" of eastern Spain.[26]

As his conquests had already magnified Jaume's proclaimed image of power, they also clarified his persona as a great lawgiver. Capping the first grueling phase of Valencian reconquest in 1238, the sovereign, declaring that it was a prime func-

---

[23] José María Font Rius, "Origenes del regimen municipal de Cataluña," *AHDE* 16 (1945): 389–529; 17(1946): 229–589; idem, ed., *Cartas de población y franquicia de Cataluña*, 2 vols. (Madrid, 1969–1983); Theresa M. Vann, "The Town Council of Toledo during the Minority of Alfonso VIII (1158–1169)," in *Medieval Iberia: Essays on the History and Literature of Medieval Spain*, ed. Donald J. Kagay and Joseph T. Snow (New York, 1997), 43–60.

[24] J. Massip, "Els origens de la administració de justicia a Tortosa des de la Carta de Població a les Costums," X *CHCA*, Comunicaciones, 1–2:461–73; José Lladonosa Pujol, "Jaime I el conquistador y la ciudad de Lérida," X *CHCA*, Comunicaciones, 1–2:449–460, esp. 455–59; Jesús Lalinde Abadía, *Los fueros de Aragón* (Zaragoza, 1979), 33–39; Jaime Caruana Gómez de Barreda, ed., *El fuero latino de Teruel* (Teruel, 1974), 31–38; Stephen P. Bensch, *Barcelona and its Rulers, 1076–1291* (Cambridge, 1995), 74–80; Antonio Aunós Pérez, *El derecho catalán en el siglo XIII* (Barcelona, 1926), 199, 272; Donald J. Kagay, "Two Towns Where there was Once One: The Aldea in Medieval Aragon," *Mediterranean Studies* 6 (1996): 29–38, esp. 36–37.

[25] Karen Kennelly, C.S.J., "Catalan Peace and Truce Assemblies," *Studies in Medieval Culture* 5 (1975): 41–51; idem, "Sobre la paz de Dios y sagrera en el condado de Barcelona (1030–1130)," *AEM* 5 (1968): 107–36; Eugen Wohlhaupter, *Studien zur Rechtsgeschichte Göttes- und Landfrieden in Spanien* (Heidelberg, 1933), 76–101, 129–35; Andrè Debord, "The Castellan Revolution and the Peace of God in Aquitaine," in *The Peace of God: Social Violence and Religious Response in France around the Year 1000*, ed. Thomas Head and Richard Landes (Ithaca, NY, 1992), 135–64.

[26] Thomas N. Bisson, "The Organized Peace in Southern France and Catalonia, ca. 1140–ca.1230," *AHR* 82 (1977): 290–303, esp. 291; Maravall, *Estudios*, 1:100–6.

tion of his office to enact "good customs," issued a code for all his Valencian lands.[27] This collection of laws, the *Furs*, as well as those established for Aragon in 1247, the *Fueros*, were "national" in that they applied to all inhabitants of an entire territory, and were organized with an apparatus of book, title, and chapter which owed much to the influence of Roman law.[28] With the proliferation of a university-trained bureaucracy that had drafted the new laws and saw them evolve into royal policy, the conservative forces of Jaume's lands, spearheaded by the Aragonese and Valencian barons, rose up in rebellion against the hated "innovations" which the new laws represented.[29] To mollify his great men who distrusted modern, Romanist administration, the king on two separate occasions, forswore the use of Roman law or advocates trained in it within his court system.[30] Unsatisfied with what they saw as a halfway measure on the part of the king, the barony of Aragon took the offensive and, with the formation of a political and military institution, the *Unión*, altered the legislative direction of the entire Crown of Aragon for the next century.[31] In this maelstrom of bold regalist assertions

---

[27] Manuel Dualde Serrano, ed., *Fori Aniqui Valentiae* (Madrid, 1950–1967), 2–3.

[28] Gunnar Tilander, ed., *Los fueros de Aragón* (London, 1937), 3–4; Lalinde Abadía, *Fueros de Aragón*, 54–62; E. M. Van Kleffens, *Hispanic Law Until the End of the Middle Ages* (Edinburgh, 1968), 240–41.

[29] Jesus Lalinde Abadía, "Ordenamiento interno de la Corona de Aragón en la época de Jaime I," X *CHCA*, Ponencias, 186–97; idem, *La jurisdicción real interior en Cataluña ("Corts, Veguers, Batlles")*, (Barcelona, 1966), 199–201; Lope Rogelio Pérez Bustamente, "El gobierno y la administración de los territorios de la Corona de Aragón bajo Jaime I el Conquistador y su comparación con el regimen de Castilla y Navarra," X *CHCA*, Comunicaciones, 1–2:515–32; Antonio M. Aragó and José Trenchs Odena, "Las escribanías reales catalano-aragonesas de Ramón Berenguer IV a la minoría de Jaime I," *RABM* 80 (1977): 421–42.

[30] *LF*, 2:300–1, chaps. 399–400; Kagay, "Structures," 66–67; idem, "The Emergence of 'Parliament' in the Thirteenth-Century Crown of Aragon: A View from the Gallary," in *On the Social Origins of Medieval Institutions: Essays in Honor of Joseph F. O'Callaghan*, ed. Donald J. Kagay and Theresa M. Vann (Leiden, 1998), 223–41, esp. 231–32; Angel Canellas López, "Fuentes de Zurita. '*Anales*, III: 66–67': Las asembleas de Calatayud, Huesca y Ejea en 1265," *Cuadernos del historiador Jeronimo Zurita* 31–32 (1981–1982): 12–41.

[31] *CAVC*, I, pt. 1:137–38, nos. 1–3; Luis González Anton, *Las uniones aragonesas y las Cortes del reino, 1283–1301*, 2 vols. (Zaragoza, 1975), 1:365–491; Joseph F. O'Callaghan, "Kings and Lords in Conflict in Late Thirteenth-Century Castile and Aragon," in *Iberia and the Mediterranean World in the Middle Ages*, ed. Paul Chevedden, Donald Kagay, and Paul Padilla (Leiden, 1996), 117–35; Esteban Sarasa Sánchez, *Sociedad y conflictos sociales en Aragón XIII–XV siglos (Estructuras de poder y conflictos de clase)* (Madrid, 1981), 33–74; Ferrando Valls

countered by equally impassioned baronial pronouncements, Pere Albert, an important member of the Barcelona chapter, lived out his career as one of Jaume I's most trusted legists.

Roman Law and Government in the Thirteenth-Century Crown of Aragon

If, as Joseph Strayer asserts, one of the great accomplishments of the Middle Ages was the sketching of the faint outlines of the nation state, then, as Alan Watson and Fredric Cheyette contend, this change towards a more professional and stable way of government can largely be attributed to the men who made law and shaped judgements from it.[32] Until the twelfth century, this ordering of power was largely carried out on the local level by great lords whose castellated might could advance, in some ways, to the level of kings.[33] The dominance of the periphery would continue largely uncontested until the twelfth century, when sovereigns across Europe started to define themselves in the political terms delineated in the *Code* of Justinian. The transformation of the royal image had its roots in the emergence of Roman law studies which spread from epicenters in Provence and at Bologna to touch virtually all European regions. The "reception" of the technology of imperial law, much like that of the personal computer in the later twentieth century, was accomplished through a symbiosis of a potent legal system with men who saw unlimited career possibilities in its manipulation.[34]

Taberner, "Los abogados en Cataluña durante la Edad Media," idem, *Obras*, 2:281–318, esp. 286–87.

[32] Joseph R. Strayer, *On the Medieval Origins of the Modern State* (Princeton, 1970), 8–9; Alan Watson, *The Evolution of Law* (Baltimore, 1985), 118; Cheyette, "Invention of the State," 162–70.

[33] Pierre Bonnassie, "Du Rhône a la Galicie: Génèse et modalités du régime féodal," in *Structures féodales et féodalisme dans l'Occident méditerranéen X\<e\>–XIII\<e\> siècles: bilan et perspectives de recherches* (Rome, 1983), 17–55, esp. 21–23; idem, *From Slavery to Feudalism*, 107–9; Theodore Evergates, *Feudal Society in the Bailliage of Troyes under the Counts of Champagne, 1152–1284* (Baltimore, 1975), 151–52; idem, "Nobles and Knights in Twelfth-Century France," in *Cultures of Power: Lordship Status and Procession in Twelfth-Century Europe*, ed. Thomas N. Bisson (Philadelphia, 1995), 11–35, esp. 29–35.

[34] For influence of Roman law in the later Middle Ages, see André Gouron, "La science juridique française aux XIe et XIIe siècles: Diffusion du droit de Justinien et influences canoniques jusqu'à Gratien," in idem, *Études sur la diffusion des doctrines juridiques médiévales* (London, 1987), 22–23; J. F. T. Plucknett, "The Relations between the Roman Law and

The acceptance of the "new law" of Rome throughout Europe was inextricably tied to the emergence of the university and, as such, followed very similar lines of transmission across the Continent. In the Crown of Aragon, the pace of Roman influence was accelerated by the happenstance of geopolitics. By two seemingly unconnected events — the marriage of Ramon Berenguer III (1097–1131) to the heiress of Provence in 1110 and that of Pere I to the heiress of Montpellier in 1202 — Catalonia and the rest of eastern Spain were firmly connected by dynasty and government to the prime centers of legal studies in southern France.[35] The *studium generalis* of Bologna also became a magnet for Iberia's students who, like their fellows across Europe, came "in crowds" to sit at the feet of such masters as Irnerius at Bologna and Placentius at Montpellier.[36] In both centers, the Spanish became an important section of the university's ultramontane guild of scholars.[37] When the graduates from these schools returned to commence careers in their homelands across the Pyrenees, they brought back with them all the standard texts of Roman law which eventually found their way into the great clerical libraries of Catalonia and Aragon.[38]

---

the English Common Law down to the Sixteenth Century. A General Survey," *University of Toronto Law Journal* 3 (1939–1940): 24–50, esp. 32; Quirinius Breen, "The Twelfth-Century Revival of Roman Law," *Oregon Law Review* 24 (1944–1945): 244–85; Hans Julius Wolff, *Roman Law: An Historical Introduction* (1951; repr. Norman, OK, 1976), 188; Knut Wolfgang Nörr, "Institutional Foundations of the New Jurisprudence," in *Renaissance and Renewal in the Twelfth Century*, ed. Robert Benson and Giles Constable (Cambridge, MA, 1982), 324–38; Charles Duggan, "Papal Judges Delegate and the Making of the 'New Law' in the Twelfth Century," in *Cultures of Power*, 172–202; Charles Homer Haskins, *The Renaissance of the Twelfth Century* (Cambridge, MA, 1927; repr. New York, 1976), 193–223.

[35] *GCB*, 7, chap. 4; *CSJP*, 49–50, 59, chaps. 31, 34; O'Callaghan, *Medieval Spain*, 218, 249; Bernard F. Reilly, *The Medieval Spains* (Cambridge, 1993), 107.

[36] Antonio García y García, "La penetración del derecho clásico medieval en España," *AHDE* 36 (1966): 575–93, esp. 579–80.

[37] Eduardo de Hinojosa y Naveros, "La admisión del derecho romano en Cataluña," in idem, *Obras completas*, 3 vols. (Madrid, 1948–1974), 2:391–92; L. J. Daly, S.J., *The Medieval University* (New York, 1961), 69–70; Joaquím Miret i Sans, "Escolars catalans al estudi de Bolonia en la XIIIª centúria," *BRABLB* 8 (1915): 137–55; Bloch, *Feudal Society*, 1:116–17; Hastings Rashdall, *The Universities of Europe in the Middle Ages*, ed. F. M. Powicke and A. B. Emden, 3 vols. (Oxford, 1895; repr. Oxford, 1997), 1:156; 2:13, 121.

[38] André Gouron, "Aux origines de l'influence des glossateurs en Espagne," in idem, *Études sur la diffusion*, 338–41; *Usatges*, trans. Kagay, 23–24; Kagay, "Emergence of 'Parliament'," 231–32.

At the end of a long train of legal events from the eleventh century onward that slowly altered the old Spanish March from a personal to a territorial regime of law, the imperial codes were less a catalyst for such change than a theoretical blueprint by which it could be accomplished.[39] Since the new universities taught their graduates to view the study of law as a "science" rather than an unconnected collection of customs, Roman law was seen as an intellectual system that existed as a "rational, universal, and centralized" influence[40] on any customary regimen it might encounter.[41] From the second half of the twelfth century, the relationship of Roman law to "the usages of the land" (*usaticos terrae*) was theoretical, supplementary, and regalist.[42] As a system the practitioners of which exerted massive efforts to render it into a "coherent whole,"[43] Roman law served as a jurisprudential textbook for custom that addressed topics which were beyond the purview of local law. The coherence of the *Code* soon recommended it as a supplement for the municipal codes of Tortosa and Lérida and the territorial legislation of Majorca and Valencia.[44]

Besides its value as a kind of legal veneer for the pockmarked face of custom, the "new law" also provided a cogent model of centralized royal power. Throughout Europe, "sovereigns and jurists often entered into a very successful alliance"[45] in both shaping the law and the Crown's relationship to it. The influence of Roman law and of a new class of legal experts can clearly be seen in Cata-

[39] Simeon L. Guterman, *From Personal to Territorial Law* (Metuchen, NJ, 1972), 1–34; Norman Zacour, *An Introduction to Medieval Institutions* (New York, 1976), 122–27; Pierre Riché, *Daily Life in the World of Charlemagne*, trans. Jo Ann McNamara (Philadelphia, 1973; repr. Philadelphia, 1983), 11–13.

[40] Paul H. Freedman, "Catalan Lawyers and the Origins of Serfdom," *Mediaeval Studies* 48 (1986): 288–314, esp. 291.

[41] Breen, "Twelfth-Century Revival," 285; G. C. J. J. van den Bergh, "The Concept of Folk Law in Historical Context: A Brief Outline," in *Folk Law: Essays in the Theory and Practice of 'Lex Non Scripta'*, ed. Alison Dundes Renteln and Alan Dundes, 2 vols. (Madison, WI, 1994), 1:11–12; Manlio Bellomo, *The Common Legal Past of Europe, 1000–1800*, trans. Lydia G. Cochrane (Washington, DC, 1995), 43–44.

[42] *Usatges*, trans. Kagay, 25; José Balari Jovany, *Orígenes históricos de Cataluña*, 2 vols. (1899; Abadía de San Cugat, 1964) 2:491.

[43] Donahue, "Law, Civil," 7:420.

[44] Rafael Altamira y Crevea, "Spain," in *Continental Legal Series*, 11 vols. (New York, 1968), 1:646; Hinojosa y Naveros, "Derecho romano en Cataluña," 2:395–96; Freedman, "Origins of Serfdom," 292.

[45] van den Bergh, "Concept of Folk Law," 1:13.

lonia's first great code, the *Usatges of Barcelona*. These laws, which first came into existence in the mid-twelfth century, tried to bring order to feudal relations, while amplifying the sovereignty of two political titles long associated with the count of Barcelona: "prince" (*princeps*) and "ruler" (*potestas*).[46] In the century after the *Usatges'* first appearance, Roman law was increasingly used to define what the office of sovereign was or should be. Like his fellow Christian rulers across Europe, the Count of Barcelona "recognized no superior" in his own lands and was above all forces except the rule of God and law. As both the father and son of law, the monarch had a central duty to maintain "right order"[47] in his realm with the establishment of peace and justice for all his subjects.[48] With such regalist doctrines to guide them, the first faint outlines of central government began to solidify in the corps of university-trained experts who were "armed with letters and learning."[49] Lawyers became so essential to the vision and functioning of governance that, as Matthew Paris observed, kings kept them "as a huntsmen keeps hounds."[50]

Of the large group of Iberian students who matriculated in the universities of Montpellier, Toulouse, and Bologna, a fairly high percentage stayed on in the academic world to attain advanced degrees, and then took up teaching as a profession. Of this group, some like the great canonists Raymond de Penyafort, Vincentus, and Laurentius of Spain as well as the older and younger Bernardo of Compostella, became famous as authors and professors.[51] A far greater number of the

---

[46] *Usatges*, trans. Kagay, 33–39.

[47] O'Callaghan, *Learned King*, 29.

[48] Ernst H. Kantorowicz, *The King's Two Bodies: A Study in Medieval Political Theology* (Princeton, 1957; repr. Princeton, 1981), 120–21, 150, 155; James M. Blythe, *Ideal Government and the Mixed Constitution in the Middle Ages* (Princeton, 1992), 31–32; Walter Ullmann, *The Medieval Idea of Law as Represented by Lucas of Penna* (New York, 1969), 66; Kenneth Pennington, *The Prince and the Law, 1200–1600: Sovereignty and Rights in the Western Legal Tradition* (Berkeley, 1993), 92–93; John Hudson, *The Formation of the English Common Law: Law and Society in England from the Norman Conquest to Magna Carta* (London, 1996), 27; Maravall, *Estudios*, 1:98–99, 119; Berman, *Law and Revolution*, 118–19; Francisco Elías de Tejada, *Las doctrinas políticas en la Cataluña medieval* (Barcelona, 1950), 179–83.

[49] Carolly Erickson, *The Medieval Vision: Essays in History and Perception* (New York, 1976), 135.

[50] Erickson, *The Medieval Vision*, 137.

[51] García y García, "Penetración," 582–83; Brundage, *Medieval Canon Law*, 196–97, 201, 222–23; Cyril E. Smith, *The University of Toulouse in the Middle Ages* (Milwaukee, WI, 1958), 207; Pedro Vidal, *Anales de la Orden de Predicadores, 1172–1228,* Biblioteca Univer-

Spaniards trained in "both laws" (*ius uterque*) returned home after their education was completed and made careers in their homelands. The most important of these were Vidal de Cañellas, Guillem de Sala, Guillem Botet, Pere Botet, and Ponç de Lleida.[52] Though active in clerical, municipal, and royal circles, they would surely agree with the sixteenth-century chronicler, Jeronimo Zurita, who characterized them as: "men . . . who prided themselves on being experts in legal science, and in civil and canon laws."[53] Many of these new lawyers returned to the clerical institutions that had largely underwritten their education. Though a good number of these professionals remained in minor orders as members of cathedral chapters, some entered the monastic and mendicant orders whose growing wealth and position made it prudent to have lawyers on staff.[54] Even while these advocates carried out their clerical duties, many also served in *ad hoc* or permanent posts of royal administration. This corps of lawyers on both sides of the Pyrenees served Jaume I as both judges ordinary of his own court or judges delegate for specific cases. The king increasingly turned to these experts for the drafting and editing of such legislation as the Valencian *Furs* and Aragonese *Fueros*.[55] Those "learned in law"[56] were also in constant demand among the eastern Spanish municipalities and business communities. In this sphere, they were instrumental regulating the

---

sitaria de Barcelona, MS. 748–49, fol. 270; F. Balthasar Sorío, O.P., *De viris illustribus Provinciae Aragoniae Ordinis Predicatorum* (Valencia, 1950), 34–38.

[52] Valls i Taberner, "Abogados," 310–16; Elías de Tejada, *Doctrinas políticas*, 178.

[53] Robert I. Burns, S.J., "Canon Law and the Reconquista: Convergence and Symbiosis in the Kingdom of Valencia under Jaume the Conqueror (1213–1276)," in *Proceedings of the Fifth International Congress of Medieval Canon Law* (Vatican City, 1980), 387–424, esp. 389.

[54] García y García, "Penetración," 582; José María Font Rius, "El desarrollo general del derecho en los territorios de la corona de Aragón (siglos XII–XIV)," in *VII Congrés de història de la corona d'Aragó* [VII *CHCA*], 3 vols. (Barcelona, 1963–1964), 1:289–326, esp. 296.

[55] Hinojosa y Naveros, 2:392–94; Guillem María de Broca y Montagut, "Juristes y jurisconsults catalans del segles XI, XII y XIII: Fonts del seus coneixements y transcendència," *Anuari* 2 (1908): 429–42, esp. 433–36; Ricardo del Arco y Garay, "El famoso jurisperito del siglo xiii, Vidal de Cañellas, obispo de Huesca (noticias y documentos inéditos)," *BRABLB* 8 (1916): 464–80, 508–21, 546–50; idem, "Nuevas noticias biográficas del famoso jurisperito del siglo xiii, Vidal de Cañellas, obispo de Huesca," *BRABLB* 9 (1917): 221–49; 10 (1921): 83–113.

[56] Aunós Pérez, *Derecho catalán*, 170.

world of commerce and shipping in such codes as the *Consolat de Mar*.[57] The diffusion of Roman law that these men embodied was readily apparent in the spread of the new concepts of jurisprudence and the books which contained them throughout the literate public of the Crown of Aragon by the dawn of the fourteenth century.[58]

In the midst of the vast array of lawyers serving the church, crown, and municipalities of the thirteenth-century Crown of Aragon stands the life and career of Pere Albert. It is not unlikely that Pere Albert inherited from the same source his position in the Barcelona chapter as well as his training in Roman law. In the first decade of the thirteenth century, a Barcelona canon named Albert was listed among the Spanish students pursuing a degree at Bologna.[59] While this "master Albert" indeed might be the author of the *Customs of Catalonia*, there is no conclusive evidence for this. Instead, we have several snippets of documentation open to a number of different interpretations. In 1233, Pere Albert "canon of Barcelona" acted as a guarantor for the repayment of a loan by "my grandfather" (*avus meus*). Our sources do not reveal if this relative, named Ferrario de Guenata, had any connection to the Master Albert of the Bolognese records.[60] Pere Albert's family connection through the Barcelona chapter, however, clearly continued into the later years of the thirteenth century with the career as Barcelona cathedral

---

[57] Burns, "Canon Law," 389–92; Berman, *Law and Revolution*, 349–56; Bensch, *Barcelona and its Rulers*, 380; Fernando Valls i Taberner, "Notes sobre el 'Consolat de Mar'," idem, *Obras*, 2:177–87; idem, "Ordinacions navals catalanes del segle XIV," idem, *Obras*, 2:198–200. For the later medieval increase of lawyer influence in Barcelona, see James S. Amelang, *Honored Citizens of Barcelona: Patrician Culture and Class Relations* (Princeton, 1986), 69–73; Richard L. Kagan, *Lawsuits and Litigants in Castile, 1500–1700* (Chapel Hill, NC, 1981), 128–63.

[58] García y García, "Penetración," 587–88; Gouron, "Science juridiques," 8–10; Bellomo, *Common Legal Past of Europe*, 63–65; Nörr, "Institutional Foundations," 327–28. For the spread of lawbooks into general educated circles of Catalonia in the later Middle Ages, see Antonio Rubió i Lluch, *Documents per l'història de la cultura catalana mig-eval*, 2 vols. (Barcelona, 1908–1921), 1:71, 98–99, 103–4, 141–42, 152–53, docs. 63, 81, 87, 136, 149; Arcadio García Sanz, "El 'Corpus juris civilis' en els documents dels segles xii–xiv," *Ausa* 6 (1969): 89–102.

[59] Bensch, *Barcelona and its Rulers*, 380.

[60] Arxiu de la Catedral de Barcelona [hereafter ACB], Pergamins, Diversorum D=C, no. 3248.

canon of Paschal Albert. Paschal, Pere Albert's brother, also served as an advocate and judge delegate in Jaume I's courts.[61]

Aside from these hints about his past, the only real light thrown on Pere Albert comes from the records of his long legal career. From 1233 to 1263, the Barcelona canon remained one of Jaume I's favorite judges, deciding cases concerning land disputes, differences over feudal tenure and the inheritance of fiefs, repayment of debt, dowries, and the level of revenues that laymen owed clerical institutions.[62] Because of his trusted position as loyal servant to the crown, Pere Albert was also occasionally called on to serve the king as a diplomatic agent. The most important example of this occurred in 1259 when the Barcelona canon, along with several other clerics headed by the bishop of Gerona, opened the secret marriage negotiations which eventually saw the crown prince Pere wedded to the strong-willed Hohenstaufen heiress Constanza.[63] In his position as a king's man, Pere Albert appeared in the royal court on a fairly regular basis. As such, he was called on to witness such official documents as Jaume's promise in 1258 that he would not devalue the principal Catalan currency.[64] The Barcelona canon, however, sometimes seemed to bridge the civil and religious worlds in which he operated. Thus in December 1236, as a public servant and one of the eminent members of the Barcelona chapter, he was present at Montpellier and witnessed the king's oath of homage and fealty to the bishop of Angoulême.[65] The canon's "free and devoted service" (grata et devota servicia)[66] was never forgotten by the sovereign. Indeed, with Jaime's support, Pere Albert seems to have acquired a

---

[61] ACA, Pergaminos de Jaime I, no. 1721. Both Petrus Albertus and Paschalus Albertus, referred to as "canonici Barchinone," are listed as witnesses of this document.

[62] ACB, Pergamins, Diversorum A, no. 2311; Diversorum D=B, nos. 1184, 7106; ACA, Pergaminos de Jaime I, nos. 1035, 1241, 1684. See also Linda A. McMillin, "Sacred and Secular Politics: The Convent of Sant Pere de les Puel·les in Thirteenth-Century Barcelona," in Iberia and the Mediterranean World, 235.

[63] Diccionari Biogràfic [hereafter DB], 4 vols. (Barcelona, 1966), 1:39; Soldevila, Pere, 1:90–93; E. L. Miron, The Queens of Aragon (London, 1913), 111–12.

[64] Joaquím Miret y Sans, Itinerari de Jaume I "el Conqueridor" (Barcelona, 1918), 279.

[65] Ambrosio Huici Miranda and Maria Desamparados Cabanes Pecourt, eds., Documentos de Jaime I de Aragón [hereafter DJ], 5 vols. (Valencia, 1976–1988), 1:391–92, doc. 241; Miret i Sans, Itinerari, 125–26.

[66] ACA, Real Cancillería, R. 9, fol. 48; DJ, 3:297, doc. 841; Miret i Sans, Itinerari, 279.

number of properties, the most important of which was near the Castell-nou and the Jewish quarter and along Barcelona's oldest street, the *Call*.[67]

In addition to his career as a royal judge and confidential agent, Pere Albert also acted as legal and ecclesiastical representative (*vicarius*) of the bishop of Barcelona and of his chapter. The most important of these missions was that of proctor to the provincial Council of Tarragona in 1249. One of the last references we have to Pere Albert, not as a legal agent of the Crown, but solely as a member of the Barcelona chapter, is from a signature list of witnesses to an arbitrated settlement between two Catalan clerics in May, 1259.[68]

From the foregoing, it can be concluded that the 1230s and 1240s constituted the height of Pere Albert's career, an era during which he probably completed the bulk of the *Customs of Catalonia*.[69] Despite the dearth of personal information about Pere Albert's later years, the dossier of his professional activities throws light on the life of a man whose legal education and practical adjudicative experience helped to fuel "the era of advanced effervescence in the development of Roman and canon law"[70] which took place during the long reign of Jaume I and afterward.[71] Like Guillem Botet, Jaume Bellvis, Vidal de Cañellas, Jaume Callis, Narcis de Sant Dionis, Françesc Bonet, and a host of other Catalan lawyers down to the sixteenth century, Pere Albert used his knowledge of the law to fashion a multi-faceted career as administrator, judge, advocate, and legist.[72]

The Legal Conundrum of Catalan Feudalism

Catalonia, the northeastern section of Spain which radiates out from Barcelona, came into being in the wake of the catastrophic destruction of the Visigothic realm and the almost-as-rapid ascendance of the Carolingian empire. With the conquests of Charlemagne (768–814) and his son, Louis the Pious (814–840), between 778 and 814, Barcelona and its hinterland were converted into the Span-

---

[67] For Jewish quarter, the *Call*, which stretched from the Castell-nou to the central cathedral, see T. N. Bisson, *The Medieval Crown of Aragon. A Short History* (Oxford, 1986), 78; Bensch, *Barcelona and its Rulers*, 34, 87; Francesc Carreras i Candi, *Geografia general de Cataluña, La ciutat de Barcelona* (Barcelona, 1916), 17.

[68] ACB, Pergamins, Diversorum D=B, no. 754; D=C, no. 7106.

[69] *Constitucions de Catalunya*, 21–26; Broca y Montagut, "Juristes," 436–38.

[70] Burns, "Canon Law," 389.

[71] Font Rius, "Desarrollo," 296

[72] *Constitucions de Catalunya*, 21–26; Broca y Montagut, "Juristes," 436–38.

ish March (*limes, marca hispanica*), a Carolingian outpost against Muslim *Hispania*.[73] This zone, soon bristling with the castles that would eventually give the region its name, was divided into counties which stretched from the Pyrenees along the courses of the Segre, Llobregat, Ter, and Fluvía rivers.[74] Ruled by "official nobles" who stood for a distant Carolingian emperor, eastern Spain remained "a society of free men" until the steady devaluation of Carolingian power after Charlemagne's death in 814.[75] With the "militarization" of Catalan life during this era, the regime of feudal relations began to take shape.[76]

As the tenth century dawned, the Catalan counts, though constantly asserting their authority by referring it back to a decadent Carolingian empire, could not compete with the local dominance of the castellans. Public structures generally faded, to be replaced by the bonds forged between individuals. The centers of this largely uncentered world were the castle and the fief. To garrison the many fortresses which dominated Catalan town and country, the counts, local nobles, and even churchmen gave temporary "control" (*potestas*) of these outposts to "castellans" (*castellani, castlans*). The basis of castellan power was the "castellany" (*castellania*) that included the fortress itself, a determined zone of territory and customary revenues which could be exacted from the inhabitants of these lands. The castellan divided the appurtenances of the castle into a number of "knight's fees" (*caballariae, feva*), and with these supported a company of men who essentially served as the castle garrison.[77]

---

[73] Derek W. Lomax, *The Reconquest of Spain* (London, 1978), 13, 33; Roger Collins, *The Arab Conquest of Spain, 710–797* (London, 1989), 210–16.

[74] Ramón d'Abadal i de Vinyals, *Els primers comtes catalans* (Barcelona, 1958; repr. Barcelona, 1983), 121–55; Bonnassie, *From Slavery to Feudalism*, 168.

[75] Pierre Bonnassie, "A Family of the Barcelona Countryside and its Economic Activities Around the Year 1000," in *Early Medieval Society*, ed. Sylvia Thrupp (New York, 1967), 103–27, esp. 108–11; idem, "Sur la formation del féodalisme catalan et sa première expansion (jusqu'à 1150 environ)," in *La formació i expansió del feudalisme català*, ed. Jaume Portella i Comas (Gerona, 1985–1986), 7–21, esp. 9–10; idem, *From Slavery to Feudalism*, 152–53, 156.

[76] Archibald Lewis, *The Development of Southern French and Catalan Society, 718–1050* (Austin, 1965), 238–39; idem, "Cataluña como frontera militar (870–1050)," *AEM* 5 (1968): 15–29, esp. 26–27.

[77] Thomas N. Bisson, "Feudalism in Twelfth-Century Catalonia," in *Structures féodales*, 172–92, esp. 173–75; Pierre Bonnassie, *La Catalogne du milieu du XIe à la fin du XIe siècles: Croissance et mutation d'une société*, 2 vols. (Toulouse, 1975–1976), 2:739–43.

Besides this set of castle holdings, there existed another means of tying allegiance to tenure, the "fief" (*fevum, honor*). In this form, a "vassal" (*vassalus, homo*) swore "with righteous faith and without deceit" to support and serve his "lord" (*dominus, senior*); the lord, in turn, swore to protect his man and reinforced this relationship by granting land or revenues to him. Though the bond born in the "oath of homage and fealty" (*sacramentum, fidelitas, hominiaticum*) was crafted in terms of loyalty and even affection, nothing prevented a vassal from taking more than one lord.[78] This vassalic desire for security was soon matched by a lordly desire for order. Thus was born "ligeance" (*solidancia*), which consisted of a vassal's prime allegiance to "a best lord above all others."[79] When even this form began to proliferate beyond manageable levels into "a system of crossed allegiance," the regime of Catalan lords and vassals was forever altered by the emergence of the "public" aspirations of the count of Barcelona.[80]

The "recreation" of public power in the Spanish March was a development marked by both daring and conservative actions. Starting with the reign of Ramon Berenguer I (1035–1076), the "official" ruler of the counties of Barcelona, Gerona, and Ausona began to reclaim his old Carolingian jurisdictional base while monopolizing such new avenues to power as general legislation and a war of reconquest against Muslim *Hispania*.[81] With the momentous reign of Ramon Berenguer IV (1131–1162), these trends of comital advancement coalesced with the stunning defeats of the Muslim *tā 'ifa* states of Tortosa and Lerida between 1148 and 1150.[82] When Ramon Berenguer married Petronilla, the heiress of Aragon,

---

[78] Josep Trenchs Odena, "La escribanía de Ramón Berenguer III (1097–1131): Datos biográficos," *Saitabi* 31 (1984): 1–36, esp. 36; *Usatges*, trans. Kagay, 120; Bisson, "Feudalism," 176–77; idem, "The Problem of Feudal Monarchy: Aragon, Catalonia and France," *Speculum* 53 (1978): 466–78, esp. 402–3; Poly and Bournazol, *Feudal Transformation*, 64–73; R. van Caenegem, "Government, Law and Society," in *Cambridge History of Medieval Political Thought*, 174–210, esp. 204–5.

[79] Bonnassie, *Catalogne*, 2:743–48; idem, "Formation," 15; idem, *From Slavery to Feudalism*, 159; Joseph R. Strayer, "Feudalism," in *DMA*, 5:52–57, esp. 55.

[80] Poly and Bournazel, *Feudal Transformation*, 73.

[81] Bisson, "Problem of Feudal Monarchy," 406–9; idem, "The Organized Peace in Southern France and Catalonia, ca.1140–ca.1230," *AHR* 82 (1977): 290–303, esp. 296–300; Bishko, "Reconquest," 3:404–7.

[82] David Wasserstein, *The Rise and Fall of the Party-Kings* (Princeton, 1985), 285–87; Caffaro, *De captione Almerie et Tortuose*, ed. Antonio Ubieto Arteta (Valencia, 1973), 30–35; Bishko, "Reconquest," 409–11; Lomax, *Reconquista*, 93.

in 1137, he fulfilled his regal aspirations — at least for his son.[83] These martial and matrimonial triumphs doubled the territory that owed allegiance to the count of Barcelona and enhanced his reputation with the addition of a royal title.[84]

Such political advances could hardly fail to change the perception and reality of feudal relations at all levels of Catalan society. This change was nowhere more apparent than in Catalonia's first great law code, the *Usatges of Barcelona*. In these laws, which first appeared in the early 1150s, the potestative claims of the count of Barcelona were coupled with an ordering of feudal relationships within the ranks of the Catalan nobility.[85] The creators of the *Usatges* made no attempt to bring into being a unified "feudal system" nor place the count of Barcelona at the head of a "feudal pyramid." Instead, the diffuse nature of Catalan feudalism was broadly channeled within a regalist structure built around the office of the count of Barcelona. The result of this evolving political solution, marked by a constant tension between a unifying center and a defiant periphery, was "a conservative provincial society transformed . . . yet not overwhelmed by a feudalism distinctly her own."[86] As a fief holder in his own right and in the name of the Barcelona chapter, Pere Albert knew firsthand the anomalies of feudal relations in Catalonia, even though he occasionally attempted to define and explain them with the vocabulary and ideology of Roman law.

This rectification of feudal norms, most especially in regard to the fief, had long been carried out by the literate servants of the crown. Following the trends of document-based government sponsored by the Carolingians, lords and vassals in the old Spanish March and afterwards relied on written "pacts" (*convenientiae*) to delineate the relationship of duties and expectations which bound the two parties.[87] Even at the lowest levels of Catalan society, the written proof of feudal

---

[83] Joaquím Traggia, "Illustración del reynado de don Ramiro de Aragón," *MRAH* 3 (1799): 497–592, esp. 588–91; Josep Pererna Espelt, "Les condiciones de la unió de Aragó i Catalunya en un manuscrit de Valencia Rafael Martí de Viciana," *Arxiu de Textos Catalans Antics* 2 (1983): 357–61.

[84] Aunós Pérez, *Derecho catalán*, 50–51; José María Font Rius, "La comarca de Tortosa a raiz de la reconquista cristiana (1148)," *CHE* 19 (1953): 104–28.

[85] *Usatges*, trans. Kagay, 33–44.

[86] Bisson, "Feudalism," 192.

[87] Bonnassie, *Catalogne*, 2:739–40, 748–49; Eulalia Rodón Binué, *El lenguaje técnico del feudalismo en el siglo XI en Cataluña: Contribución al estudio de latín medieval* (Barcelona, 1957), 184; Rosamond McKitterick, *The Carolingians and the Written Word* (Cambridge, 1990), 60–75.

ties became a standard feature in the relations between lord and vassal. They became so widespread that many notaries possessed sample feudal pacts that could be adapted simply by filling in the names of the parties.[88] Though the bond of homage may have begun as a link between two men or, at most, between two sets of retainers, it soon evolved beyond the tidy imagination of the law. The count of Barcelona and other lords, fearing that feudal service would be undermined, repeatedly attempted to stop the transfer of feudal lands and revenues by laymen to clerical institutions. Yet bishoprics, monasteries, and crusading orders held castles and fiefs from the count of Barcelona and other lords. In turn, they granted these to knights and peasants alike. With this feudal mingling of the clerical and noble "orders," it was not unheard-of for bishops and abbots to serve as feudal lords who held as their vassals the count of Barcelona and other members of the Catalan barony.[89] Eventually, the feudal bond permeated the ranks of the clergy itself, with chapters and monastic communities standing as vassals to their lords among the ranks of bishops and abbots. The hybrid nature of such arrangements is apparent among many of the clerical corporations which regularly designated procurators to tend to feudal duties.[90] Much the same arrangement existed with town councils which, as corporations, stood as lords or vassals.[91] As the status and nature of parties bound to feudal conventions changed, so did the duties which these agreements called for and the medium in which they were carried out. Thus by the mid-fourteenth century it was quite usual for salaried officials to swear fealty "in accordance with the *Usatges of Barcelona*" to civil or ecclesiastical lords, who were, in effect, their employers. No fiefs were granted the vassal/employee; instead, in exchange for the "faithful" performance of his duties, the vassal was paid the salary and other revenues that accrued to his office. The same method was also used to see that royal officials or parliamentary commissioners

---

[88] Johannes Vincke, ed., *Documenta Selecta Mutuas Civitatis Arago-Cathalaunicae et Ecclesiae Relationes Illustrantia* [hereafter *DS*] (Barcelona, 1936), 499–500, doc. 651; *Usatges*, trans. Kagay, 120, app. 3, doc. 5.

[89] Bisson, "Problem of Feudal Monarchy," 467.

[90] José Rius Serra, ed., *Cartulario de Sant Cugat del Vallès* [hereafter *CSCV*], 3 vols. (Barcelona, 1945–1947), 3:201–2, 384–85, 399–400, docs. 1032, 1264, 1282; Federico Udina Martorell, ed., *El "Llibre Blanch" de Santes Creus* (Barcelona, 1947), 2–3, doc. 2; Miret i Sans, *Itinerari*, 133; *DJ*, 2:33–34, doc. 267.

[91] *DS*, 498–99, doc. 650; J. N. Hillgarth and Giulio Silano, eds., *The Register "Notule Communium 14" of the Diocese of Barcelona (1345–1348)* [hereafter *Notule*] (Toronto, 1983), 117, doc. 281; Donald J. Kagay, "Royal Power in an Urban Setting," 127–36.

would carry out their duties "faithfully, legally, and well without any hatred, fear, partisanship, or any kind of corruption whatsoever."[92]

While the character of feudal relations in Catalonia slowly seemed to change, an essential binding agency among all sorts of groups remained, even when they exercised few of the duties originally associated with the *convenientia*. Though homage was to tie lord and vassal in a permanent relationship that could be terminated only by a formal vassalic "defiance" (*diffidamentum*), Jaume I and his successors normally viewed such action as treason.[93] Though such heartfelt differences between offended lords and contumacious vassals long remained a feature of the Catalan feudal landscape as shown by the sad fate of two royal vassals — Jaume III of Majorca and Bernat de Cabrera — in 1343 and 1364 respectively, homage often seemed more of a bother than a flashpoint.[94] Lords became exasperated with a growing trend among their men of postponing the homage and fealty ceremonies, even when this brought down on them their lord's anger and a sizeable penalty.[95]

The spread of the use of homage and fealty throughout Catalan society was accompanied by the Crown's insistence on determining the actual extent of feudal land in Catalonia and then making sure that the boundaries of each fief were

---

[92] *Notule*, 249–52, 295, docs. 41, 73; *DS*, 61, doc. 108; *CAVC*, 2:249.

[93] Donald J. Kagay, "The Iberian *Diffidamentum*: From Vassalic Defiance to the *Code Duello*," *The Final Argument: The Imprint of Violence on Society in Medieval and Early Modern Europe*, ed. Donald J. Kagay and L. J. Andrew Villalon (Woodbridge, Suffolk, 1998), 73–82, esp. 73–75; idem, "Violence Management in Twelfth-Century Catalonia and Aragon," in *Marginated Groups in Spanish and Portuguese History*, ed. William D. Phillips, Jr. and Carla Rahn Phillips (Minneapolis, 1989), 11–21, esp. 13–14; Miret i Sans, *Itinerari*, 503; Walter Ullmann, *The Individual and Society in the Middle Ages* (Baltimore, 1966), 64–65; R. C. van Caenegem, "Law and Power in Twelfth-Century Flanders," in *Cultures of Power*, 149–71, esp. 152.

[94] Pere III, *Crònica*, trans M. Hillgarth, ed. J. N. Hillgarth, 2 vols. (Toronto, 1980) 1:240–43, chaps. 13–14; 2:544, 556–58, chaps. 40–46; Rafael Tasis i Marca, *Pere el Ceremoniós i els seus fills* (Barcelona, 1980), 31–33, 42–45; J. E. Martinez Ferrando, *La tràgica història dels reis de Mallorca* (Barcelona, 1975), 204–7; J. B. Sitges, *La muerte de D. Bernardo de Cabrera, consejero del rey d. Pedro IV de Aragón* (Madrid, 1911), 34–38; Donald J. Kagay, "The 'Treasons' of Bernat de Cabrera: Government, Law, and the Individual in the Late Medieval Crown of Aragon," *Mediaevistik* 13 (2000): 39–53. Both men were charged with *bausia*, treason occasioned by vassalic insubordination.

[95] *DS*, 216–17, 377–78, 510–11, docs. 317, 511, 665; *DJ*, 2:80–81, doc. 315; *Notule*, 112, 125, docs. 297, 307.

acceptable to the vassal who held it and to his neighbors. Besides the danger attendant on assigning any boundaries, such determinations were made even more difficult because of the survival of vast swaths of allodial territory in both the original Spanish March (Old Catalonia) and in the lands conquered in the twelfth century (New Catalonia).[96] While such freeholds were very often turned into fiefs, feudal land could also change its status: Pere Albert himself altered the terms under which his land near the Jewish quarter in Barcelona was held.[97] As a result, the legal limit between feudal and allodial land blurred. It was not unusual for notaries to refer to "feudal property" (res feodalis) held allodially "in full and free ownership."[98] Such confusions were deepened when a fief was subdivided among several vassals or sold through several hands.[99] Since any land could be enfeudated, sites not normally associated with feudal tenure, such as towns and cities, were given as fiefs, and then might be subdivided among other vassals.[100] One example — and not an atypical one — was Tarragona, which in the course of the twelfth century saw itself divided among its original lord, two bitter vassalic rivals, and a town council.[101]

Despite the difficulties of determining what land was feudal in medieval Catalonia and who had the right to it, sovereigns from Alfons I (1162–1196) stepped into the breach. The first attempt at such record-keeping and its immediate effect

---

[96] van Caenegem, "Government, Law, and Society," 206–7; Evergates, Feudal Society, 131–32; Bisson, "Problem of Feudal Monarchy," 465–66; Font Rius, "Comarca," 113–14; Ramon Marti, "La integració a l'alou feudal de la seu de Girona de les terres beneficiades pel 'regim dels hispans': Els casos de Bàscara i Ullà, segles IX–XI," in Formació, 49–62.

[97] CSCV, 1:19, doc. 17; 3: 131, doc. 949. Pere Albert apparently sold part of this fief to Maria, wife of G. Jordan, and her daughters and then opened a "street" (callem) through the fief which he gave to "certain Jews" who held the property as lessees (in emphiteosim). For transfer of allodial to feudal lands and viceversa in France, see Theodore Evergates, trans., Feudal Society in Medieval France: Documents from the County of Champagne (Philadelphia, 1993), 7–9, 53, doc. 7, 36 B–C.

[98] DJ, 3:298, doc. 841; Notule, 197, doc. 544; Odilo Engels, Schutzgedanke und Landesherrschaft im ostlichen Pyrenaenraum (9.–13. Jahrhundert) (Munich, 1970), 223.

[99] "Llibre Blanch," 185, doc. 184; Miret i Sans, Itinerari, 207–8; DJ, 2:361, doc. 546.

[100] DJ, 1:341, doc. 204; Miret i Sans, Itinerari, 113.

[101] ACA, Pergaminos de Ramón Berenguer IV, no. 243; Marca hispanica, 1313–14, doc. 417; Francisco Miguel Rosell, ed., Liber Feudorum Maior [hereafter LFM], 2 vols. (Barcelona, 1945–1947), 1:262–65, doc. 247; Lawrence J. McCrank, "Norman Crusaders in the Catalan Reconquest: Robert Burdet and the Principality of Tarragona, 1079–1155," in Medieval Frontier History in New Catalonia (Aldershot, 1996), no. IV, 67–82.

in escalating royal control took place in the late 1170s, when a royal notary acquired — surely by purchase — a great number of feudal documents. These were eventually organized chronologically and territorially into the *Liber Feudorum Maior*.[102] Much the same effect was attained, at least initially, in the *repartimientos*, the division of the lands which accompanied the conquests of Majorca, Valencia, Jativa, and Murcia.[103] With the rapid influx and movement of settlers, no list for either allodial or feudal land, except a regularly-updated census, could adequately organize ownership information for the new territories. The tale of one such settler, Prince Pedro of Portugal, demonstrates the fluidity of fief-holding in the era of the great conquests.[104] With fiefs being exchanged, sold, divided, mortgaged, and granted as parts of dowries or wedding gifts, questions over their tenants or the extent of their revenues increased greatly during the thirteenth century and often required settlement in a royal court. The touchstone of dispute in

---

[102] Thomas N. Bisson, "Ramón de Caldes (c.1135–c.1200): Dean of Barcelona and King's Minister," in *Law, Church and Society: Essays in Honor of Stephan Kuttner*, ed. Kenneth Pennington and Robert Somerville (Philadelphia, 1977), 286–87; idem, "Feudalism," 187–89; Anscari M. Mundó, "El Pacte de Cazola de 1179 i el 'Liber Feudorum Maior': Notas Paleogràfiques i Diplomàtiques," X *CHCA*, Comunicaciones, 1–2:119–29. For a masterful discussion of how the *Liber* came into being, see Lawrence J. McCrank, "Documenting Reconquest and Reform: The Growth of Archives in the Medieval Crown of Aragon," in idem, *Medieval Frontier History*, no. I, 305–18.

[103] Luis García de Valdeavellano y Arcimus, *Curso de historia de las instituciones españoles de los origines al final de la edad media* (Madrid, 1968), 242–43; Robert Bartlett, *The Making of Europe: Conquest, Colonization and Cultural Change 950–1350* (Princeton, 1993), 139–48. See also *Colección de documentos inéditos del Archivo General de la Corona de Aragón* [hereafter *CDACA*], ed. Próspero Bofarull y Moscaró, 42 vols. (Barcelona, 1850–1856), vol. 11.

[104] *DJ*, 1:379–80, doc. 235; Miret i Sans, *Itinerari*, 78–79, 96, 103–4, 123, 169, 194; Felipe Mateu y Llopis, "El infante don Pedro de Portugal, *Dominus Regni Maioricarum*," *BRAH* 173 (1976): 239–46; Luis Adao da Fonseca, "Contribución para el estudio de las relaciones diplomaticas entre Portugal y Aragón en la Edad Media: El tratado de alianza de 1255," X *CHCA*, Comunicaciones 1–2, 547–56, esp. 553. The Portuguese prince, Pedro, uncle of King Sancho II (1223–1245), spent most of his adult life in the service of Jaume I. In 1229, he was named the "lord of the Kingdom of Majorca" (*dominus Regni Maioricarum*). Four years later, he married the widowed countess of Urgel, Aurembaix, and with her death in 1236, fell heir to all of her lands on both sides of the Pyrenees. In 1244, he traded these Majorcan and Urgelese titles for the important Valencian cities of Segorbe, Castellon de la Plana, Murviedro and Almenara. Pedro also served as an intermediary between the Portuguese and Aragonese crowns.

litigation most often centered on the extent to which a vassal could alienate such lands and revenues without his lord's permission.[105]

As the influence of feudal relations widened in Catalan society, the status of the region's castles also began to change. The castellany and knight's fee remained, but the terms which bound lord to castellan were clearly influenced by the feudal *convenientia*. An increasing number of castles were thus held as fiefs.[106] Regardless of the name applied to the castle tenure, it imposed on the castellan much the same military obligation as in the twelfth century and granted him a similar base of fiscal support.[107] The crown, throughout the late twelfth and thirteenth centuries, attempted to alter the conditions under which castles were held, converting them in the process from a fiscal liability to an asset. Castle control, in a sense, had become a commodity that brought ready cash into the hands of a sovereign always strapped for money. To assert their authority directly over castles, Jaume I and his immediate successors increasingly appointed their administrators and private servants as castellans. These grants were often temporary ones made to repay debts or reward loyal service. The new class of castellans paid an annual fee to the crown and then proceeded to reimburse themselves from the revenues attached to the fortress.[108] While Catalan castles were not generally entrusted to Muslim castellans, as often was the case in the new lands conquered from Islam, neither were all the fortresses of Catalonia under the direct control of the crown.[109] Many were held by clerical and noble lords who exercised a conservative, yet extremely efficient exploitation of the castle hinterland.[110]

Although the building of castles slowed during the era of the great conquests

---

[105] *CSCV*, 3:199–201, 400, docs. 1081, 1283; *DS*, 511, doc. 666; Miret i Sans, *Itinerari*, 211, 233.

[106] Bisson, "Feudalism," 190–91; Miret i Sans, *Itinerari*, 207.

[107] *CSCV*, 3:494, doc. 1376; "*Llibre Blanch*," 19–20, 27–28, docs. 16, 22; *DJ*, 1:199, doc. 105; 2:294, doc. 482.

[108] *DJ*, 2:146, 235–36, docs. 360, 438; 3:17–18, doc. 559; Robert I. Burns, S.J., *Diplomatarium of the Crusader Kingdom of Valencia: The Registered Charters of the Conqueror Jaume I, 1237–1276* [hereafter *Diplomatarium*], 3 vols. to date (Princeton, 1991–), 2:67, 150, 180, docs. 75ª, 178ª, 211.

[109] Robert I. Burns, S.J., *Islam under the Crusaders: Colonial Survival in the Thirteenth-Century Kingdom of Valencia* (Princeton, 1973), 308–10; María Teresa Ferrer i Mallol, "La frontera meridional valenciana durant la guerra amb Castella dita del Dos Pere," in *Pere el Cerimoniós i la seva època*, ed. María Teresa Ferrer i Mallol (Barcelona, 1989), 260–75.

[110] Thomas N. Bisson, "The Crisis of Catalan Franchises (1150–1200)," in *Formació*, 157–63.

and such construction was largely limited to royal fortresses, the definition and transfer of castle titles and conditions of tenure remained as fluid as those of other fiefs of the era.[111] Like feudal properties, castles could be subdivided between parties, one part being considered allodial and the other feudal. Though the share of revenues was divided among the castle tenants by the initial granter (normally the king), these could be limited to the lifetime of the tenant. He might maintain some of these dues for himself, or restrict the kind of economic activities his tenants could engage in.[112] It was more normal, however, for these funds to pass down to the tenant's descendants.[113] Castle titles could also be sold or exchanged; in such transactions, the terms and protections which applied to the site remained in effect despite the change in tenancy.[114] When such changes took place in castles held by multiple lords and staffed by more than one castellan, transition proved exceedingly difficult and very often led to violent disputes.

According to the *Usatges*, the lord of a contumacious vassal could confiscate the "rebel's" castle and all fiefs attached to it. The offended lord could hold these until he was compensated by the offender.[115] In his long reign, Jaume I repeatedly went through this process with Christian and Muslim vassals, all of whom experienced a royal vengeance sanctioned by custom.[116] When the issues were not as desperate or the involved parties were clerics or women, royal justice stepped in to provide arbitration. Such decisions were not always accepted, and the "pacifications" (*pacificationes*) which terminated the suits might provide raw material for new rounds of violence.[117]

---

[111] *DJ*, 3:100, doc. 620; Miret i Sans, *Itinerari*, 223. For royal ban against building new castles or possessing royal artillery without royal possession, see *Usatges*, trans. Kagay, 82–83, art. 73; Donald J. Kagay, "The Use and Misuse of 'Prohibited Arms' in Frontier Texas and Medieval Iberia," *Lamar Journal of the Humanities* 22 (1996): 5–18.

[112] *CSCV*, 2:331–32, doc. 668; *DJ*, 3:20–21, doc. 561.

[113] *Diplomatarium*, 2:348–49, doc. 405ª; *DJ*, 2:306–7, doc. 496; Miret i Sans, *Itinerari*, 138, 197.

[114] "*Llibre Blanch*," 391–94, doc. 391; *DJ*, 1:202–3, doc. 108; 2:233–35, doc. 437; Miret i Sans, *Itinerari*, 73, 182.

[115] *Usatges*, trans. Kagay, 71, art. 26.

[116] *CSCV*, 3:61, doc. 864; *Diplomatarium*, 2:84–85, doc. 47ª; Kagay, "Baronial Dissent," 64; Paul E. Chevedden, "The Artillery of King James I the Conqueror," in *Iberia and the Mediterranean World*, 79–80; Paul Douglas Humphries, "Of Arms and Men: Siege and Battle Tactics in the Catalan Grand Chronicles," *Military Affairs* 49 (1985): 173–78.

[117] *DS*, 316, doc. 436; Miret i Sans, *Itinerari*, 284; *Marca hispanica*, 1219–20, doc. 326; Kagay, "Violence Management," 14–16.

Tenancy of castles was not the only issue that spurred violence, litigation, or both. As a core of revenues and pledged responsibilities, the castle jurisdictions were fertile ground for differences about how much service a castle lord or castellan could demand and how long the neighboring vassals or garrison could defer in carrying out a wide array of duties. The non-payment of castle revenues caused the bitterest recriminations. When these made their way before royal justice, the king and his judges were more than willing to allow the castle lord to deal with the matter "as ... [he] saw fit." This normally meant taking over the castle by force.[118] In more complicated matters, like the settlement of revenue levels after the sale or exchange of a castle, royal judges were called in to render a settlement.[119]

Service and submission, in one form or another, were other major components of the castellany or knight's fee, which also caused nagging, sometimes violent, exchanges. According to the *Usatges*, castellans had some "judicial rights" (*estaticum, estatje*) over the surrounding populace and could make a "moderate use" of the castle hinterland.[120] The most important issues spawned by the uncertain relationship of the castellan to the surrounding populace were (1) the imposts collected to support the castle's military viability; (2) the kind of labor which could be enforced to support the castle; and (3) the territorial limits for expeditions emanating from the castle. Like royal officials, the castellan could collect from his constituencies a number of taxes, including the *redemptio exercitus*, a payment made in lieu of army service. When these taxes crossed the line of custom, they could be resisted on the grounds that they were "arbitrary exactions" (*questias*).[121] Many of the castle residents and those living in surrounding lands — both freeholders and feudatories — were bound to provide labor gangs for castle upkeep. During sieges, the castellan's demand for such units might pass customary limits, causing the populace to clamor for the resolution of their grievances.[122] As garrisons became more difficult to raise, castellans emerged as "middlemen" of sorts, who used royal grants as a substitute for knights' fees by hiring a company of knights who served as a garrison and answered any royal call for military service in the district

---

[118] *DJ*, 2:73, doc. 309; *Diplomatarium*, 2:154–55, doc. 185.

[119] ACA, Pergaminos de Jaime I, no. 1035; *Diplomatarium*, 2:184–85, doc. 217ᵃ.

[120] *Usatges*, trans. Kagay, 89, art. 97.

[121] *Diplomatarium*, 2:156–57, doc. 187ᵃ; Donald J. Kagay, "Army Mobilization, Royal Administration and the Realms in the Thirteenth-Century Crown of Aragon," in *Iberia and the Mediterranean World*, 95–116, esp. 102–3.

[122] *DS*, 32, 508, docs. 60, 661; Kagay, "Army Mobilization," 104–5.

for a limited time.[123] The unspecified temporal and territorial limit of such service would both constitute the basis of a number of individual suits and feed into the broader issues of national military obligations.[124]

In general terms, Catalonia, until the end of the twelfth century, was — as Bisson has called it — a limited "feudal monarchy."[125] As the crown sought to organize the diffuse comital regime of the old Spanish March into a unified territorial realm, royal justice attempted to smooth away the complicated anomalies of a Catalan feudalism growing ever more complex. The difficulties of this mission were heightened in a land "with a feudal soul" but an increasingly non-feudal body.[126] At the core of this effort stood the corps of royal advocates, judges delegate, and legists. An important member of this group was Pere Albert.

The Corpus of Pere Albert: Aspirations and Failures

In the struggle between the old scholarly orthodoxy concerning feudalism and the current view that no "system" is to be gleaned from the surviving evidence of homage and feudal contract, the decisions and treatises of late twelfth and thirteenth-century lawyers on feudal matters are either fully accepted as the makings of a "second feudal age" and "feudal principality"[127] or are completely rejected as the basis of an intellectual construct which was incorrect at its inception and sowed the seed of this falsehood with every succeeding generation of scholars.[128] The truth, however, lies somewhere between these two positions and cannot be arrived at without an even-handed assessment of the several generations of lawyers who attempted to make some judicial sense of the feudal world in which they lived. To shed a clearer, less prejudiced light on the adjudicative and jurisprudential implications of the professional activities of such advocates, Pere Albert's major

---

[123] *Diplomatarium*, 2:38, 247, docs. 42ª, 289ª; Miret i Sans, *Itinerari*, 532.

[124] Miret i Sans, *Itinerari*, 478, 525–26.

[125] Bisson, "Feudalism," 190.

[126] Burns, *Islam*, 274.

[127] Marc Bloch, "European Feudalism," in *Theories of Society: Foundations of Modern Sociological Theory*, ed. Talcott Parsons et al., 2 vols. (New York, 1965), 2:385–92; idem, *Feudal Society*, 1:59–60; Joseph R. Strayer, "Feudalism in Western Europe," in *Feudalism in History*, ed. Rushton Coulborn (Hamden, CT, 1965), 15–24, esp. 19; *The History of Feudalism*, ed. Herlihy, 197–98; Sidney Painter, *Mediaeval Society* (Ithaca, NY, 1951), 16–17.

[128] Reynolds, *Fiefs and Vassals*, 478.

work, the *Customs of Catalonia*, must be better understood in its own immediate Catalan and broader European setting.

The starting point for the study of Pere Albert's work clearly lies with the *Usatges of Barcelona*, the first major statement of feudal and territorial law in Catalonia. Created by the "Romanizing lawyers" of Ramon Berenguer IV's court, the code, which would not attain a general acceptance in Catalonia until the thirteenth century, tied together a great number of laws and customs around two nuclei: the ordering of the feudal relations with the establishment of a hierarchy of homage and the definition of the Count of Barcelona's sovereignty. Far from being a blueprint for royal dominance, the *Usatges* sought to maintain a separation of function between the arenas of feudal and monarchical power. Unlike the perfect "feudal pyramid" so often cited in European historiography and so little seen in European records, the situation visualized in the *Usatges* was more akin to largely autonomous cellular growth, limited principally by the narrowing of the medium on which such development was taking place. The disparate nature of the code was perhaps its strongest point: it gave living space to both royal government and feudal relations. The *Usatges*, however, did not stint on theory, but neither did it attempt to over-define the customary norms of feudalism. Its lack of a full explanation of the workings of homage and fealty as well as its incomplete discussion of castle and feudal tenure did induce Pere Albert, a working advocate and judge, to fill in the gaps in policy and practice which the authors of the *Usatges* may have purposefully left unaddressed.

The provenance of Pere Albert's work can be discerned only indirectly from the work itself. In article 39, the Barcelona canon lays out a hypothetical case to illustrate the tenuous boundary between feudal and royal allegiance. Though he peoples this example with such nebulous, unspecified figures as the count of Empuriés and Aimery, viscount of Narbonne, Pere Albert does give his hypothetical case an identifiable location, the kingdom of Valencia. Jaume I began to refer to himself as "king of Aragon, Majorca, and Valencia" from October 1238. In the same period, documentary evidence of the "city and kingdom of Valencia" (*civitatis et regni Valentiae*) also began to emerge. The boundaries of the new kingdom were laid out in its law code, the *Furs*, which was probably issued in 1238. Valencia's southern boundary was established with the Jativa campaign of 1244.[129] With these dates in mind, we can assume (although cannot categorically prove)

---

[129] *DJ*, 2:45, doc. 277; *Fori*, 1; Robert I. Burns, S.J., *The Crusader Kingdom of Valencia: Reconstruction of a Thirteenth Century Frontier*, 2 vols. (Princeton, 1967), 1:7–9.

that the Barcelona canon composed the *Customs of Catalonia* between 1238 and 1244.[130] Not surprisingly, this era also comprises the busiest period of Pere Albert's career as ecclesiastical and civil advocate.

Despite these clues, Pere Albert's work has little in common with the flurry of legislation in Jaume I's lands between 1228 and 1277. Unlike the municipal codes of Lerida and Tortosa and the great royal collections, the *Furs* of Valencia and the *Fueros* of Aragon, the *Customs of Catalonia* contains as transmitted neither introductory statement of purpose nor organizational apparatus.[131] Like the *Usatges*, it was not a code written to be immediately enacted into law. Unlike the *Usatges*, it made no attempt to attribute itself to an earlier era, nor did it claim any author but Pere Albert, whose name remained associated with the work until it was officially accepted as Catalan law in the fifteenth century.[132] Thus, whether the *Customs of Catalonia* was a working version of a project which Pere Albert's busy public life did not allow him to complete or a notebook of sorts to aid in the adjudication of the various types of feudal cases that came before him as judge delegate must remain an open question. The text of *Customs of Catalonia*, like that of the *Usatges*, was divided into separate articles, each dealing with a distinct legal problem. These fall into two classes: a delineation of Catalonia's customary law in regard to whatever subject Pere Albert was analyzing or a more detailed statement of a case involving feudal relations and how they should be adjudicated according to Catalan law. The general subjects dealt with in the *Customs of Catalonia* were: (1) the extent of royal sovereignty attached to the office of the count of Barcelona; (2) the ceremony of homage by which lords were bound to vassals and the actions that would lead to the rupture of such ties; (3) the sale, transfer, inheritance, and division of the fief; (4) the sale and transfer of castle tenancies; and (5) the nature of the castellan's office and its jurisdictional relationship to castle garrisons and the populace living in the fortress hinterland.

For subsequent Catalan political theory, the most significant articles of the *Customs of Catalonia* were those which expanded the section of the *Usatges* with the incipit *Princeps namque*.[133] This article declared that when the count of Barcelona

---

[130] *Constitucions de Catalunya*, ciii.

[131] Aunós Pérez, *Derecho catalán*, 199; Arco y Garay, "Vidal de Cañellas," 466–72; Font Rius, "Desarrollo," 304–6; Van Kleffens, *Hispanic Laws*, 240–41; Burns, "Canon Law," 397–99.

[132] *DB*, 3:41.

[133] For later Catalan political theory, see Elías de Tejada, *Doctrinas políticas*, 138–213; Ferran Valls i Taberner, "Les doctrines politiques de la Catalunya medieval," idem, *Obras*,

was faced with a foreign invasion, he could call out all of his subjects to aid him and, despite their relationship to the invader or to other feudal lords, they had to help him "since no man must fail the ruler in such a great matter and crisis."[134] Pere Albert worked from this simple statement of a subject's duty to his sovereign to explore its implications in the world of feudal relations. He thus put the following question: when was a vassal, regardless of his allegiance to his lord, bound to serve the king and when could he refrain from doing so? To determine the key to this vexing query, the canon first explored the well-worn concepts of "public utility" and "regnal status" to show the difference between public and private power.[135] To recognize the difference, he relied on the Roman legal concepts of "jurisdiction" (*jurisdictio*) and "authority" (*imperium*).[136] His solution, which sprang from the Romanist dictum "public utility must be preferred to private," was an extremely clever — though not wholly original — bit of reasoning. He declared that during a national emergency the king's authority, even over liege vassals, was greater than that of their lords. In this case, with the king possessing "pure authority" (*merum imperium*) and the lord "aggregate authority" (*mixtum imperium*), the vassal would have to stand against his lord, and even against his own father, rather than failing in his duty to the king.[137] This was, however, not a statement of absolute royal power on Pere Albert's part for when there was no national crisis, the jurisdiction which the lord wielded over his vassal was greater than the king's authority.[138] This argument, which still surfaces in battles be-

---

2:210–16; Donald J. Kagay, "*Princeps namque*: Defense of the Crown and Birth of the Catalan State," *Mediterranean Studies* 8 (1999): 1–32.

[134] *Usatges*, trans. Kagay, 80, art. 64. For similar concept in Visgothic and Carolingian law, see *LV*, 370–78, IX, 2, 8; Alfred Boretius and Alfred Kraus, eds., *Capitularia Regnum Francorum*, MGH., Regum. sectio II, 2 vols. (Hanover, 1907), 1:134.

[135] Strayer, *Medieval Origins*, 26; Ullmann, *Individual and Society*, 34–39.

[136] Berman, *Law and Revolution*, 289–91; John W. Perrin, "Azo, Roman Law and Sovereign European States," *Studia Gratiana* 15 (1972): 92–101. For similar views among such contemporaneous thinkers as Jean de Blanot and Jacques de Revigny, see Pennington, *Prince and the Law*, 96, 102–3.

[137] For this same test of authority to determine which of two jurisdictions was the more important at any one time, see *Notule*, 159, doc. 425.

[138] Joan de Socarrats, *In Tractatum Petri Alberti canonici Barchinonensis de consuetudinibus Cataloniae inter dominos et vassalos ac nonnullis aliisque Commemorationes Petri Alberti appellantur* [hereafter Socarrats, *Commemorationes*] (Barcelona, 1551), 404–5, 417–18; Josep Rovira i Ermengol, ed., *Los Usatges de Barcelona y els Commemoracions de Pere Albert* (Barcelona, 1984), 184–88; Maravall, *Estudios*, 149–56.

tween individual rights and a state's eminent domain, was extremely important in later medieval Catalan political thought, especially that spawned with the growing influence of Castile in eastern Spain initiated with the era of the Catholic Kings.[139]

One of the clearest gaps in the feudal laws of the *Usatges* centered on how feudal relations were initiated or terminated. Ligeance, one of the most significant developments of the twelfth century, was barely discussed.[140] In the *Customs of Catalonia*, this feudal norm was fully dealt with. Tying homage to a lessening of one's status by decree in Roman legal terms, Pere Albert then gives a clear description of the rite by which homage was carried out. As in other parts of Europe, the ceremony included the "mixing of hands" (*inmixtio manuum*) and the "kiss" (*osculum*).[141] The Barcelona canon also tried to lay out the guidelines of ligeance (one of the most contentious issues which came before him as a judge), but was never fully able to unravel this confusing form. Distinguishing liege from non-liege homage by determining the extent of jurisdiction and authority that a lord held over a vassal, Pere Albert declared that such a vassal "totally binds . . . his legal identity to his lord."[142] Following the argument evinced to determine the border between feudal suzerainty and royal sovereignty, he declared that because ligeance implied a "general jurisdiction" of a lord over a vassal, "no one can render liege homage to two lords."[143] Logically correct as this statement might have been in Romanist terms, it scarcely represented a Catalan feudal reality marked by the steady proliferation of ligeance. Though not retreating from his logical ruling on *solidancia*, Pere Albert did not try to provide means by which the fiction of only one "best lord" for each "best vassal" could be maintained, while working out the troublesome reality of one vassal with two liege lords inconsiderate enough to wage war on each other.[144]

---

[139] Bisson, *Medieval Crown*, 141–43, 157–59.

[140] *Usatges*, trans. Kagay, 69, 72, 75, arts. 20, 33, 54.

[141] Socarrats, *Commemorationes*, 324; Rovira i Ermengol, ed., *Usatges*, 174–75. For other European descriptions, see *History of Feudalism*, ed. Herlihy, 98, doc. 15; Bloch, *Feudal Society*, 1:146–49; Galbert of Bruges, *The Murder of Charles the Good*, trans. James Bruce Ross (Toronto, 1959; repr. Toronto, 1988), 206–8, chap. 56.

[142] Socarrats, *Commemorationes*, 445; Rovira i Ermengol, ed., *Usatges*, 195; *Usatges*, trans. Kagay, 72–73, art. 33.

[143] Socarrats, *Commemorationes*, 304; Rovira i Ermengol, ed., *Usatges*, 171.

[144] Socarrats, *Commemorationes*, 317, 349; Rovira i Ermengol, ed., *Usatges*, 172–74, 181–82; Bloch, *Feudal Society*, 1:211–18.

Regardless of the extent of feudal jurisdiction, homage, for Pere Albert, was sealed when the lord invested his vassal with land. In most cases, except for extremely small fiefs, the vassal was bound to render homage to the original lord or his successors within the determined period of a year and a day.[145] If he failed to do so, the vassal might lose his fief until he rendered homage and paid a fine. Though he could follow the strategy of prescriptive claim (that is, asserting that because feudal service had not been rendered for a long period it could not be properly claimed by the lord), Pere Albert advised against this tactic, since the feudal contract that tied lord to vassal had to be rendered whenever requested.[146] Unfortunately, even this clear statement was subject to interpretation. Thus, if a lord required the military service of his vassal in an unusual expedition "to distant places," this exceeded the customary limits of armed service and the vassal would have to be paid for his involvement.[147] The close bond between homage and fief could thus encumber the fief and the vassal who held it with the crimes of the lord who had granted it. Though such unusual circumstances might disqualify a son from acceding to his father's fief, the normal rule was that a vassal's fief was inherited by the son, daughter, or relative designated as successor. These new vassals had to do homage to the lord within the proper time limits.[148] Once he rendered homage for these properties, the vassal could not abandon his fief or the duties it represented without his lord's permission. Before he did homage to his lord, however, the vassal could leave his fief behind, resigning all of its lands and revenues to the lord.[149] Yet once homage was rendered, the vassal gained only a partial control of his fief and was always under the eminent supervision of his lord. Vassalic land, then, could not be subinfeudated without the permission of the lord. Despite the prodigious legal complexities such activity caused, lords were often in favor of such subdivisions, since they charged a sizeable "fief-transfer fee" (*laudemium*) for each transaction of this type, even when it was in the vassal's family.[150]

---

[145] Socarrats, *Commemorationes*, 258, 265–66, 282, 570; Rovira i Ermengol, ed., *Usatges*, 168–71. This norm is connected to that in the *Libri Feudorum*, bk. II, tit. 26 which gave the son of a deceased vassal one year to claim his father's fief [*Feudorum Consuetudines*, 505–6].

[146] Socarrats, *Commemorationes*, 334; Rovira i Ermengol, ed., *Usatges*, 175–77.

[147] Socarrats, *Commemorationes*, 353–54; Rovira i Ermengol, ed., *Usatges*, 183–84.

[148] Socarrats, *Commemorationes*, 337–38, 428–29, 439–40; Rovira i Ermengol, ed., *Usatges*, 177–81, 190–94.

[149] Socarrats, *Commemorationes*, 244, 568; Rovira i Ermengol, ed., *Usatges*, 165.

[150] Socarrats, *Commemorationes*, 543–44, 568–69.

As with homage and fiefs, the *Usatges* were often unclear about the regime of castles. The prime law of the code on this subject was that which concerned "control" (*potestas*) of the fortress. The castellan would have to surrender his custody of the castle to the lord whenever requested. Yet a fortress could normally be held for up to ten days before it had to be returned. If the castellan refused to surrender *potestas*, the lord could confiscate the fortress and hold it until the castellan reestablished homage and repaid all costs to his lord. Without the lord's approval, the castellan could not sell, subdivide, or alienate the castle or anything legally connected to it, but he could moderately use castle resources and revenues.[151] From this customary and written foundation, Pere Albert would proceed to produce a much sounder and more complicated structure.

Though the castellany was still in use during Pere Albert's time, he seldom used the term and fully expressed castle tenure in feudal terms. As with the *Usatges*, so with the *Customs of Catalonia*, the delineation of the terms of control was the core of each castle tenancy. Unlike the *Usatges*, Pere Albert's work gives a full description of the ceremony: the vassals would vacate the castle to the lord's men, one of whom would climb to the highest tower and declare the fortress to be under the new lord's control. If the castle happened to be in a ruined condition, the declaration of control was to be made from the highest point in the castle compound.[152] Within the specified period of ten days, the lord and his garrison could moderately use the supplies left in the fortress by the castellan and his men. Even if the castellan possessed allodial property within the castle limits, this could easily be associated with the complex of revenues and fiefs attached to the fortress unless the castellan was willing to prove his claim before the law.[153] Only in a case where the castellan or his men reentered the castle to reclaim it or the lord needed it for war, the castle would have to be restored to its former tenant after the ten-day period had passed.[154] Under certain conditions connected with the castellan's "default of service" (*fallimentum*), the lord could confiscate the fortress and hold it until the castellan made amends. Refusal to surrender the castle, post bond, or answer a military summons, along with desertion on the battlefield and the rupture of feudal ties, could cost the castellan the control of his fortress. If the castle was in the midst of a war zone or saw its title involved in litigation, the

---

[151] *Usatges*, trans. Kagay, 71, 89, 94–95, arts. 26, 28, 97, 118.
[152] Socarrats, *Commemorationes*, 33–34, 51; Rovira i Ermengol, ed., *Usatges*, 143–44.
[153] Socarrats, *Commemorationes*, 59, 133; Rovira i Ermengol, ed., *Usatges*, 144.
[154] Socarrats, *Commemorationes*, 87; Rovira i Ermengol, ed., *Usatges*, 147.

castellan could also be legally prevented from regaining control. Lords were not above manufacturing default emergencies to reclaim especially pivotal castles which they then might try to retain, even after the castellan had made up for his expensive *fallimentum*.[155]

The castellan could also be shunted aside if the lord wished to sell the fortress. If the buyer proved to be of a lower rank than the castellan (something that happened frequently as members of the Catalan bourgeoisie acquired feudal properties), then the sale could supposedly be nullified by the castellan's refusal to do homage or render service to the new owner.[156] If the sale was acceptable to all the involved parties, the new lord was installed by the former owner who took him to a high point of the castle and, before a group of peasants and vassals of the castle's surrounding territory, resigned his power over them, and then introduced the new lord, to whom they rendered homage "for themselves and all the others."[157]

On the stage of Catalan custom, then, the castellan was often put at a lower legal level. He, like any vassal, had to carry out for his lords all the duties specified in the *convenientia,* the most important of which was the surrender of castle control. If he refused to vacate the castle, returned within its boundaries during the ten-day period when the castle was given over to lordly use, or impeded the seignorial use of the fortress in any way, the lord did not have to return castle *potestas* to the castellan, who was now liable for default.[158] Some legal options, however, were given to the castellan. He could oppose a new castle lord on grounds that his new master might be of a lower status than he — meaning that homage was impossible since it would bring him dishonor. On some occasions, he could also use the prescriptive claim, saying he had not been called to surrender control for a period of thirty years or more.[159]

Despite the line of subservience which Catalan custom defined for the castellan, it also granted clear opportunities for the exercise of power. In certain cases, the castellan could alienate territory or revenues, holding these as a usufruct or a long-term lease (*emphyteusis*). Even the castle land that remained attached to the overlord came under the castellan's immediate control, when divided into knight's

---

[155] Socarrats, *Commemorationes,* 521, 596–98; Rovira i Ermengol, ed., *Usatges,* 201–4.

[156] Bensch, *Barcelona and its Rulers,* 142–52.

[157] Socarrats, *Commemorationes,* 73, 535; Rovira i Ermengol, ed., *Usatges,* 147.

[158] Socarrats, *Commemorationes,* 5, 42; Rovira i Ermengol, ed., *Usatges,* 143–44.

[159] Socarrats, *Commemorationes,* 62, 142–43, 159; Rovira i Ermengol, ed., *Usatges,* 145, 152–56.

fees to support the garrison.[160] The legal complications of so many families supported from the same swath of land increased exponentially with the proliferation of castellans. Though these officials were normally lieutenants of the first castellan, it was not unheard of for two castellans of equal rank to control one castle. The usual solution to this dangerous situation was an agreement to divide their roles — for example, one castellan to deal with the overlord and the other to deal with the castle population.[161] Though castles, like fiefs, were supposed to come under the control of the castellan only for his lifetime and then to be granted afresh by the overlord, heritability of castellanies and castle fiefs was the rule. If a castellan or vassal died intestate, it was incumbent on the lord to choose the new castellan from the official's deceased heirs. If these happened to be underaged children, the castle jurisdiction could be turned over to the supervision of a guardian until a male heir came of age or a female heir was married. The vicissitudes of inheritance could invest two heirs with the control of one castle. They would then proceed to divide in half the castle jurisdiction and the vassals associated with it or, as in the above-discussed case, each could assume a different role of castellan duty.[162]

The means which Pere Albert describes for the installation of castle purchaser as new lord demonstrates how many knights, peasants, vassals, leaseholders, and allodialists were connected to the fortress jurisdiction. The garrison was tied to the castellan by homage and the granting of fiefs; as such, it constituted a company of vassals who had to render to the castellan a wide array of services whenever he demanded them. The freeholders and other tenants living inside and near the castle, though not subordinated to the castellan, were subject to the protection of the castle. Thus, during the time of war, this population was commandeered for labor service on the fortress walls and the picket lines outside them. They were also used as skirmishers, lookouts, and guards. When the castle was besieged, they were required to aid the garrison in manning the castle walls. During such crises, the privileges and customary standing of this population were routinely sacrificed to the needs of the war effort, especially if there was any suspicion about its loyalty.[163]

If the exigencies of war jumbled the status relationships which emanated from the castle, legal proceedings could put tenants, castellans, and overlords at logger-

---

[160] Socarrats, *Commemorationes*, 187–88, 250; Rovira i Ermengol, ed., *Usatges*, 159, 165–67; For *emphyteusis*, see Josep María Pons i Guri, "Entre l'emfiteusi i el feudalisme (Els reculls de dret gironins)," in *Formació*, 411–18.

[161] Socarrats, *Commemorationes*, 256, 569–70; Rovira i Ermengol, ed., *Usatges*, 167–68.

[162] Socarrats, *Commemorationes*, 211, 235–36; Rovira i Ermengol, ed., *Usatges*, 163–64.

[163] Socarrats, *Commemorationes*, 159, 569; Rovira i Ermengol, ed., *Usatges*, 156–57.

heads in much the same way. When the owner of allodial property inside the castle grounds had the status of his possessions challenged by the castellan or castle lord, he could not expect a fair trial from the overlord who, being a litigant, was disqualified as judge. In all other disputes between castle tenants, however, the overlord was the competent judge.[164] Since the jurisdictions of vassals and other classes of tenants within castles were understood to be virtually stacked on top of each other, the offense or legal action of one could not fail had to affect the others. Thus if an overlord or castellan entered into litigation with his castle underlings, verdicts, bonds, and punishments would be passed through each range of tenants until the malefactor was punished or the litigant received justice.[165]

In comparison with the *Usatges*, the *Customs of Catalonia* is a practical, some would say unfinished, explanation of feudal norms and suits which might arise from them. Unlike the authors of the *Usatges* who completed their work and tried to make it more sophisticated by including citations of a great number of legal works, Pere Albert cited only the *Usatges* and the *Libri Feudorum*.[166] He mentioned Roman law, but only in very general terms. He did refer to a number of Romanist concepts, most especially the prescriptive claim. He had, however, little interest in the display of legal erudition in his work. He rather set out to determine if Catalan feudal practice contained a sufficient commonality to apply to all Catalonia. The resultant *Customs of Catalonia* stepped in where the *Usatges* chose not to tread, but still maintained an aloofness from a logical statement of a "feudal system" for Catalonia. Rather, Pere Albert recognized that Catalonia, like so many European lands that had been transformed from frontier marches into strong principalities and prosperous commercial centers, was an amalgam of feudal and allodial tenure as well as of oral custom and written law.[167]

---

[164] Socarrats, *Commemorationes*, 183–84; Rovira i Ermengol, ed., *Usatges*, 157–58.

[165] Socarrats, *Commemorationes*, 110, 130, 579; Rovira i Ermengol, ed., *Usatges*, 150–51.

[166] *Usatges*, trans. Kagay, 18–20.

[167] Burns, *Islam*, 274–75; Karen S. Nicholas, "The Role of Feudal Relationships in the Consolidation of Power in the Principalities of the Low Countries 1000–1300," in *Law, Custom and the Social Fabric in Medieval Europe: Essays in Honor of Bryce Lyon* (Kalamazoo, MI, 1990), 113–30, esp. 124–26; R. C. van Caenegem, "Galbert of Bruges," in *Law, Custom and the Social Fabric*, 89–112, esp. 103.

The Course of the Customs of Catalonia from Notebook to National Law

Unlike the *Usatges of Barcelona*, which took a circuitous, though traceable, road from a legal project of the Barcelona court to a set of laws fully accepted throughout Catalonia, Pere Albert's *Customs of Catalonia* came into the Catalan legal corpus after its composition — not after a long juridical shadow life, but from a straightforward and fairly brief connection with regnal and national codification.[168] Catalan sovereigns from Ramon Berenguer IV to Pere I made use of the *Usatges* in litigation and as one basis for a regalist philosophy that would come into full bloom with the reign of Jaume I.[169] By contrast, Pere Albert's work, which was never accompanied by a dedication to any clerical or lay patron, surely led a circumscribed existence among the judges and librarians of the monasteries and cathedral chapters of Old Catalonia. With the reigns of Jaume II (1291–1327) and his grandson, Pere III (1336–1387), which were in some ways as favorable to culture as that of the remarkable Castilian sovereign, Alfonso X,[170] Pere Albert's work became known to a much wider audience. In 1322 Jaume II paid the sizeable sum of thirty-six *sous*[171] for the illumination of a copy of the *Usatges of Barcelona* and the *Constitucions of Catalonia*, a collection of royal legislation and codes.[172] This process was apparently not finished or was a preliminary decoration, for in 1333 Jaume II's son Alfons III (1327–1336) paid the great court painter Ferrer Bassa two-hundred *sous* to "illuminate" the volume.[173] Although

---

[168] *Usatges*, trans. Kagay, 44–45.

[169] *Usatges*, trans. Kagay, 26–29; idem, "Emergence of Parliament," 231–32.

[170] Robert I. Burns, S.J., "*Stupor Mundi*: Alfonso X the Learned," in *Emperor of Culture: Alfonso X the Learned of Castile and his Thirteenth-Century Renaissance* (Philadelphia, 1990), 1–13; O'Callaghan, *Learned King*, 132–46; Salvador Claramunt, "Els Estudis Generals i la transmissió de saber," in *Pere el Cerimoniós i la seva època*, 151–60.

[171] The *solidus* or *sou*, silver coins struck at Barcelona and Jaca respectively from the twelfth to the fifteenth century. The Barcelona *sou*, the principal medium exchange for Catalonia's overseas trade, was worth one-third less than its Jacan counterpart which circulated in the much smaller area of Aragon and the western Pyrenean counties. The *denarius* or *dinar* was a copper coin of the same era, twelve of which equaled one Barcelonan or Jacan *sou* (Felipe Mateu i Lllopis, *Glosario hispánico de numismática* [Barcelona, 1940], 40, 190; Bisson, *Conservation of Coinage*, 74–75; idem, *Fiscal Accounts*, 1:304–5).

[172] Rubió i Lluch, *Documents*, 1:73, doc. 73.

[173] Rubió i Lluch, *Documents*, 1:104, doc. 88; F.-P. Verrié, "La política artística de Pere el Ceremoniós," in *Pere el Ceremoniós*, 177–92, esp. 188.

Pere Albert's work is not mentioned by name, its later connection with the *Constitucions* raises the possibility that this voucher of 1322 is one of the first indications that a basic canon of Catalan law, which undoubtedly included Pere Albert's book, was developing.

With the era of baronial unrest in Aragon (1265–1348), traditional law was called on throughout eastern Spain to bolster the positions of both a trenchant monarchy and disgruntled nobilities. Though Catalan baronial dissent did not lead to the formation of brotherhoods or *uniones* in the *Principate*, as with the Aragonese and Valencians, the law did remain a litmus test of loyalty or rebellion among the Catalan great men. Though a king who took every opportunity to expand the prerogatives of his office, Pere III soon realized that it was to his advantage to appear as the protector of Catalonia's fundamental laws. Despite the limits placed on his power by these customs, Pere swore his allegiance to them in 1337, and eventually came to see that they were more of a servant than an impediment to his sovereignty. He cited the *Princeps namque* — one of the prime sections of both the *Usatges* and *Customs of Catalonia* — on numerous occasions when he needed a general military response from the Catalans.[174] He was also able adroitly to utilize the law to his favor against his cousin, Jaume III of Majorca, whom he branded as a rebel in feudal terms for acting against "Our royal rights." When the case against Jaume III was proved in court in 1343, both the king and Catalan traditional laws were vindicated.[175] Besides Jaume's southern French and Majorcan realms, Pere also gained control of his cousin's law books. Ironically, in this confiscated cache of volumes all dedicated to Roman law, works on feudal law were conspicuous by their absence.[176]

If Pere III's reign demonstrated the significance of traditional law in Catalonia, it also underlined the need to know exactly which laws were included in Catalonia's legal canon. The desire for more and better codification of Catalan customs had already manifested itself in 1321 when Jaume II appointed boards, consisting of a noble, a townsmen and a lawyer, in each Catalan administrative district to in-

---

[174] Pere III, *Cronica*, trans. Hillgarth, 2:401, 523, 532, chaps. IV.12, VI.22, 30; *CAVC*, 2:230–55, 273–75; 3:16–31, 235–36, 286–99. Pere's overuse of *Princeps namque* after 1359 led the *Corts* to turn to its standing commitee, the *Diputació del General*, as the proper agency for the collection of military taxes and deployment of troops which the sovereign summoned for the defense of the realm.

[175] *Cronica*, trans. Hillgarth, 1:201, 203, 233, 244, chaps. II.21, 24, III.6; Bisson, *Medieval Crown*, 106–7.

[176] Rubió i Lluch, *Documents*, 1:127–28, 141–42, docs. 116, 136.

terpret existing law and to give advice on pending legislation.[177] With the growing number of royal statutes during the fourteenth century, the call for better or-
ganization of laws grew ever louder and more insistent. The drive for legislative
reform culminated under the reign of Martí I (1396–1410). In 1409, the king appointed a professional commission to establish a new code that would arrange in
a logical manner the *Usatges*, the *Customs of Catalonia* and all parliamentary legislation to that date.[178] With Martí's death in 1410 and the eventual accession of
Ferran I (1412–1416), the standard-bearer of a new dynasty, the Trastámaras, the
call for legal reform was again put to the crown. A *Corts* in 1413 requested that
"two good persons" and "an apt notary" be appointed to collect all traditional law
of Catalonia and translate it from Latin into "the vulgar Catalan tongue."[179]
Ferran responded by naming a new commission of lawyers headed by the former
Chancellor of the realm and parliamentary leader, Jaume Callis.[180] This massive
undertaking of gathering the best versions of the laws and translating them took
place under the supervision of the *Diputació*.

Although the work was completed and presented to Alfons IV (1416–1458) in
1422, it was not put into general circulation, but rather kept "hidden in the Royal
Archive and house of the *Diputació* [in Barcelona]."[181] This fact was surely due
to the king's fear of Catalonia's traditional law, which had increased in importance
since Martí I's death and the Compromise of Caspe, in 1412, by which an elec-
tion board chose a new ruler.[182] Alfons, who spent much of his life in making
good his claim to southern Italy and Sicily, was met by a simmering rebellion of
Catalonia's upper classes. These "pactists" looked on Alfons as a foreigner whose
administration was based on dangerous Castilian innovations that endangered the
two pillars of Catalan political life: the *Corts* and the traditional law. To protect
what they viewed as Catalonia's customary establishment, the pactists tried to sub-

---

[177] *CAVC*, 1, pt. 1:261, 263–64, arts. 9, 10, 17, 19.

[178] Jan Read, *The Catalans* (London, 1978), 106–8; Antoni Rubió i Lluch, "Joan I Hu-
manista i el primer periodo de l'humanisme català," *EUC* 11 (1917): 1–17; Ferran Soldevila, *Història de Catalunya*, 3 vols. (Barcelona, 1934), 1:414; Font Rius, "Desarrollo," 318.

[179] *CAVC*, 15:365; *Constitucions de Catalunya*, xviii.

[180] Broca, "Juristes," 491; *Constitucions de Catalunya*, xxi; Elías de Tejada, *Doctrinas políticas*, 180–81.

[181] Ramon d'Abadal i Vinyals, *Pere el Ceremoniós i els inicis de la decadència política de
Catalunya* (Barcelona, 1972), 171–72.

[182] Manuel Dualde and José Camarena, *El compromiso de Caspe* (Zaragoza, 1980); Esteban Sarasa Sanchez, *Aragón y el compromiso de Caspe* (Zaragoza, 1981).

ordinate the Trastámara monarchy to the conservative tether of the parliament, which itself acted within the political boundaries set by the *Usatges of Barcelona* and *Constitucions of Catalunya*. Despite the very real unrest the pactist movement unleashed on Catalonia for the next five decades, its own divisions never allowed the vision of a Catalonia ruled under a conservative constitutional framework to take place.[183]

With the domestic unrest that the fifteenth century brought to Catalonia and the rest of the Iberian Peninsula, the codification program of Catalan traditional law remained a veritable "secret history" until 1481 when Ferran II "the Catholic" (1474–1516), observing that laws did little good "if the people knew nothing about them," appointed another commission of legists who took fourteen years to upgrade the collection of 1422. In 1495, they produced the first printed edition of Catalan law, the *Constitucions y altre drets de Catalunya*.[184] After running through two subsequent updated editions of 1588–1589 and of 1704, the code, and local law throughout the old Crown of Aragon, ran afoul of a new view of political centralization which came to Spain with the accession of the Bourbon dynasty in 1715. With the publication of the *Decreto de Nueva Planta* in 1716, the Bourbon government attempted to establish one set of national laws which emanated from Madrid.[185] After over three centuries of suppression, traditional Catalan law, riding in the wake of Catalan cultural and economic nationalism, again saw the light of day in 1960 with the enactment of the *Compilación del Derecho Civil*. This code, which adopted many of the earlier laws to modern usages, may be called the first step towards Catalan autonomy in a Spanish Republic.[186]

---

[183] Soldevila, *Historia*, 2:43–44, 67, 75–77, 87–88; José María Font Rius, "The Institutions of the Crown of Aragon in the First Half of the Fifteenth Century," in *Spain in the Fifteenth Century 1396–1516*, ed. Roger Highfield, trans. Frances M. López-Morillas (New York, 1972), 172–92, esp. 172–79; Bisson, *Medieval Crown*, 141–45, 157–59. For the emergence of similar pactists ideas in nineteenth-century Spain, see C. A. M. Hennessy, *The Federal Republic in Spain: Pi y Margall and the Federal Republican Movement, 1868–74* (Oxford, 1962; repr. Westport, CT, 1980).

[184] *Constitucions de Catalunya*, lxx–lxvi.

[185] *Constitucions de Catalunya*, lxvii–lxx, cxxvii–cxxix; Armin Wolf, "Die Gesetzgebung der entstehenden Territorialstaaten," in *Handbuch der Quellen und Literatur der neueren europäischen Privatrechts geschichte*, ed. Helmut Coing, 3 vols. (Munich, 1973–1988), 1:517–800, esp. 690; José Luis Comellas, *Historia de España moderna y contemporanea (1474–1975)* (Madrid, 1985), 298–300.

[186] *Compilación del derecho civil, especial de Cataluña. Ley de 24 de Julio 1960* (Barcelona, 1984).

What the earliest Catalan attempts at codification created was not "a complete legislative system" like *Compilación de Derecho Civil*. Instead, it tied together "in an isolated and sporadic form" a vast collection of earlier codes, legal treatises, and individual royal and parliamentary statutes.[187] Thus, though the road to acceptance as national law was laid out and paved from 1495 onwards, it accommodated as many legal travelers as before. In this group was Pere Albert's *Customs of Catalonia*. From early in its history, the work was considered part of the *Constitucions de Catalunya*. In the 1422 compilation, the *Customs of Catalonia*, though largely a jurisprudential work, was coupled with such statutory norms as the peace and truce and royal legislation enacted in the *Corts*. Pere Albert's work was normally subdivided into the *Customs of Catalonia* and the nine *Cases*, in which a lord could confiscate his castle.[188] Though it was included in the legal canon, the private or academic nature of Pere Albert's work cast doubts upon its status as bona fide legislation. A number of scholars led by Jaume Callís declared that since the *Customs of Catalonia* and *Cases* had not been formally legislated, these works could not be considered law.[189] The commentator on Pere Albert's work, Joan de Socarrats, led a group which believed that since the works were written and long had been commented on by Catalan jurists, they acquired much the same character as customary law which became written statute under the auspices of the sovereign.[190] The question was rendered largely moot in 1470 at the parliament of Monzón, when the sections of the *Customs of Catalonia* that concerned castellans were formally accepted as national law, and in 1495, when the entire code entered the realm of legislation. Like the great Castilian code, the *Siete Partidas*, which had considerable influence on Catalan law, the vision of one legist had been transformed into general law, not by the immediate action of the crown or any political institution, but by the long, almost indiscernible influence of custom.[191]

---

[187] Font Rius, "Desarrollo," 317.

[188] *Constitucions de Catalunya*, xxvvii, lxix.

[189] *Constitucions de Catalunya*, civ, See also José Antonio Lalinde Abadía, *La persona y la obra del jurisconsulto vicense Jaume Callís* (Vich, 1980).

[190] *Constitucions de Catalunya*, civ–cv; José Egea Fernández and José María Gay Escoda, "Eficàcia de les normes jurídiques a la tradició jurídica catalana de la Baixa Edat Mitjana fins al Decret de Nova Planta," *Revista Jurídica de Catalunya* 85 (1979): 546–49.

[191] Ramon d'Abadal i de Vinyals, "Les *partidas* y Cataluña," *Estudis Universitaris Catalans* 6 (1912): 13–37, 161–81; Font Rius, "Desarrollo," 301; Robert A. MacDonald, "Law and Politics: Alfonso's Program of Political Reform," in *Worlds of Alfonso and James*, 182.

Manuscripts and Editions

Single manuscripts of Pere Albert's work are exceedingly rare and survived paired with other similar legal treatises. The most important of these joint manuscripts are:

Barcelona. Arxiu de la Corona d'Aragó, Incunable 49.
Barcelona. Arxiu de la Corona d'Aragó, Colección de Codigos, no. 1.
Barcelona. Arxiu Històric Municipal de Barcelona, Incunable prov. 51.
Madrid. Biblioteca Nacional, Ms. 12691.

The most important printed editions of the *Commemoracions* are:

Joan de Socarrats, *In Tractatum Petri Alberti canonici Barchinonensis de consuetudinibus Cataloniae inter Dominos et Vassalos ac nonnullis aliisque Commemorationes Petri Alberti apellantur* (Barcelona, 1551).
Josep Rovira i Ermengol, ed., *Los Usatges de Barcelona y els Commemoracions de Pere Albert* (Barcelona, 1984).
Mossen Josep Gudiol, "Traducció dels Usatges, les mes antiques constitucions de Catalunya y costumes de Pere Albert," *Anuari de l'Institut d'Estudis Catalans* 1 (1907): 285–334.

The most important editions of pre-Bourbon Catalan law are:

Constitucions y altre drets de Catalunya (Barcelona, 1495).
Constitucions y altre drets de Catalunya (Barcelona, 1588–89).
Constitucions y altre drets de Catalunya compilats en virtut de capitol de Cort LXXXII de las corts del Rey Don Felipe IV nostre senyor celebradas en la ciutat de Barcelona (Barcelona, 1704; repr. Barcelona, 1973).
Pedro Nolasco Vives y Cebria, *Traducción al castellano de los usajes y demas derechos de Cataluña*, 4 vols. (Barcelona, 1861; repr. Barcelona, 1988).
Josep M. Font Rius, ed., *Constitucions de Catalunya* (Barcelona, 1988).

Usage

Because Catalonia, from 1137, was a member of the Crown of Aragon, its sovereigns were known by both Catalan and Aragonese names and could also possess two different regnal numbers. I have chosen the Catalan names and regnal numbers as the more consistent with recent American scholarship on medieval Catalonia. In all other names and titles, I have followed the usage of Joseph O'Callaghan's *History of Medieval Spain*.

The Customs of Catalonia

between

Lords and Vassals

BY THE BARCELONA CANON, PERE ALBERT:
A PRACTICAL GUIDE TO CASTLE FEUDALISM
IN MEDIEVAL SPAIN

1

That No Limiting Legal Claim or Action of Dispossession Should Be Accepted Against Lords Who Demand Castle Control and the Posting of a Bond

If a lord demands that his vassal should give him control of a castle or a house[1] that he holds from him, or that he should post bond,[2] the vassal must carry out these things for his lord and must not refuse them for any legal excuse whatsoever, even when the claim of illegal confiscation [by the lord] could be alleged. In short, if a lord brings charges against his vassal in a tribunal over any matter which demands fealty, and the vassal claims that his lord has confiscated illegally any part of the fief or anything else and thus that he did not have to legally respond to the charges until this property was given back, in this case the

---

[1] This could refer to a fortified town house or, more probably, to a farmhouse (*mas*) which was often heavily fortified. See J. Camps Arboix, *La masia catalana* (Barcelona, 1959; repr. Barcelona, 1976).

[2] While the vassalic duty to post bonds for lords involved in litigation was mentioned in most feudal pacts, this duty, along with military service, was the most consistently avoided. In 1355, Pere III was forced to remind his counselor Pere de Montcada and the royal vicars that the oath of homage imposed distinct duties on vassals and if they did not carry out these "natural" obligations they were subject to treason charges and a sizeable fine. With the steady and general vassalic refusal to carry out the most primary of these duties, the defense of the lord and the fatherland, the fourteenth-century legist Jaume de Montjuich suggested that all Catalan males of fighting age should swear an oath and post a "bond" (*taxatio*) to carry out these formerly feudal duties. Socarrats, *Commemorationes*, 32–33; *Antiquiores Barchinonensium Leges, quas vulgus Usaticos appellat commentariis supremorum jurisconsultorum Jacobi a Monte judaico, Jacobi et Guilermi a Vallesicca et Jacobi Calici* [hereafter *ABL*] (Barcelona, 1544), fol. 123v.

1

vassal's objection can have no weight at all; for if claims are made against those things which demand fealty and from which treason[3] will result, no other defense may be accepted.[4]

2

Concerning the Way Control is Surrendered

If a lord demands from his vassal the control of his castle, it will be given in the following way. The vassal, having vacated the castle and its boundaries with all his possessions, will surrender the fortress to the lord without holding back or refusing anything. Then once the lord (or others acting for him) comes within the walls of the castle, he should direct two, three, or as many of his vassals as he wishes to climb to the top of the tower and shout out at the top of their lungs the name of their lord. From then on, the vassal will leave the castle and its boundaries; for he must not remain except by the express permission of the lord, or unless he happens to own allodial property within the boundaries of the castle itself. Otherwise, as long as the vassal remains within the castle boundaries, he is not thought to have surrendered control. According to the custom of Catalonia, he will remain a traitor as long as delays in surrendering full control.

---

[3] Although "treason" (*bausia*) was considered "the greatest crime" a vassal could commit against his lord, the crown made some attempts to stop the extra-legal badgering vassals normally underwent when simply accused of treason. Thus Alfons III ruled in 1337 that no one in Catalonia would be declared a "traitor" (*bausator*) unless "by due process of law" (*sententialiter*). Socarrats, *Commemorationes*, 182–83.

[4] Pere Albert disagrees with article 22 of the *Usatges* which declares that when a lord and vassal were involved in litigation, they had to settle their debts before the suit could procede. *Usatges*, trans Kagay, 70, art. 22.

3

Concerning Those Who Prevent the Full Surrender of Castle Control

Upon receiving castle control, the lord may freely and without any interference post as many guards as necessary to garrison the fortress. If the vassal, his agent, or anyone else prevents the lord from posting a sufficient number of guards or from changing these guards within the period of ten days,[5] the vassal is not considered to have surrendered full and free castle control nor, in this case, is the period of ten days binding on the lord. Similarly, this time period is not in effect if the vassal remains in or comes back into the boundary of the castle during these ten days. Thus this period should come into effect once control has been surrendered fully, freely, and without interference and provided the vassal does not return within the castle boundaries.

---

[5] In articles 3 and 7, Pere Albert sought to amplify two sections of the *Usatges* (arts. 26, 39) which ruled that a vassal had to turn his fief or castle over to his lord whenever requested. The vassals could claim these holdings back after ten days unless the lord needed them for war or for some other valid reason. *Usatges*, trans. Kagay, 40–41, 74, arts. 26, 39.

4

How Castle Control is Surrendered
if the Fortress is Destroyed

And if there is no tower or fortress there since the castle has been totally destroyed (as happens in many places),[6] then the lord, or another who receives control in his name, will enter the castle boundaries just as the castellan is going out from them. And then the lord should post two, three, or as many vassals of his company as he wishes on the house of any peasant or on any high wall of the castle. They then should call out at the top of their lungs the name of their lord and place on this fief a stake, a lance, or any other object of this kind as a sign that control had been received.[7]

---

[6] The question of legal responsibilities and revenues accruing even from a ruined castle was one brought by both castle lords and castle inhabitants alike. Despite differences in legal opinion, it became generally accepted in the fourteenth century that *potestas* applied even to ruined structures and allowed castle and populace living near such a fortress to aid in its rebuilding. The title to such ruined structures would often be determined by the testimony of the surrounding residents and members of former garrisons. Socarrats, *Commemorationes*, 58.

[7] An example of this transfer of castle properties is apparent in the sale of the castle of Montcada in which the seller placed a "pennant" (*pennonus*) on the wall to indicate that the structure had changed hands. Socarrats, *Commemorationes*, 172–73.

5

Concerning Possessions Found in the Castle
by the Lord When He Receives Control

And if a lord, while receiving castle control, finds some possessions of his vassal in the fortress or within its boundaries, he and his guards can keep and moderately make use of these supplies as is necessary while they hold the castle. If these supplies were not sufficient for the guards' needs, then the lord should pay their expenses. Yet the vassal is bound to reimburse the lord for these things.

6

That a Prescriptive Claim Cannot Aid in the Refusal
of Surrendering Control

Moreover, if in the surrender of castle control a vassal who does not have allodial property in any site within the castle boundary claims that he and his ancestors had never surrendered control of this castle in accordance with the customary procedure for castle control for a period of forty years or even longer, he can never base a legal defense on such a custom or even on a prescriptive claim.[8] Even if it was claimed that never in human memory had either the vassal or his ancestors ever surrendered control of this castle to another person, nevertheless, according to the custom and general observance of Catalonia, full surrender of castle control is not yet considered to have taken place in this case. If such a feudal pact should come to light, it would be contrary to the general custom and observance of Catalonia.

---

[8] The "prescriptive claim" (*praescriptio*) entered Roman law as a limiting rule or excuse which could be put forward as a reason for not carrying out a previous agreement. Socarrats rejected the prescriptive claim as applied to castle tenure and feudal obligations in the following words: "Control over a castle cannot be prescribed, even if such control was never given . . . Service for a fief can never be prescribed, even it was never rendered." Socarrats, *Commemorationes*, 143.

7

When Control Must Be Returned
and When It Must Not Be

After the period of ten days during which the lord freely received castle control, according to the ancient and long approved custom of Catalonia, he must return the castle to his vassal if he should demand it back. But before the lord has to return the castle to the vassal, he may require that his vassal render homage to him if he has not yet done so, and post bond with the lord for himself, his retainers, and for all his own vassals so that the guards that the lord posted as a castle garrison may safely return to their homes with all their possessions. If the lord suspects the vassal or his retainers or vassals of wishing to harm the guards on their return trip, he may demand these things. In general, the lord is not bound to return the castle until the vassal renders homage and posts bond.[9]

Likewise before the lord has to return the castle to his vassal, he can require from him a legal bond, unless he has already posted one. Once he receives it, the lord must return the castle without lessening its value in any way. But if the lord or his men cause damage to the castle proper or to anything within its boundaries, he must make restitution for all of this, even if control was not thought to have been yet fully surrendered.

8

When Such Control Cannot be Said to
Have Been Fully Surrendered

If, while a lord holds castle control, the castellan remains or comes within the castle boundary or if he, any of his retainers, or his vassals (whether they are armed or not, but are acting under the castellan's orders) collect — either freely or by force — any of the castle rents from the inhabitants of the fortress, then, in such a case, the ten-day time period established for the lord to hold castle control is not in effect.

---

[9] The most important case of fief confiscation for the vassal's failure to render homage or post a bond was that of 1342–1343 when Pere III took over the realms of Jaume III of Majorca. Although treason was the ultimate cause for this action, the king used his cousin's failure to render homage and post a bond to guarantee compliance as the reason for the confiscation of all his lands. Socarrats, *Commemorationes*, 74.

9

Concerning Garrison Expenses
Which Must Be Restored to the Lord

Likewise if a vassal does not fully reimburse his lord for the expenses he incurred in posting a castle garrison, the lord can demand all of these aforesaid costs from the vassal before he returns the castle to him. This is also the case if, after the lord received castle control, he found none of his castellan's property within the castle or its boundaries to meet the expenses of garrisoning the fortress and of supporting himself and his guards. Then the castellan is bound to reimburse these costs before the lord has to return the castle to him. But if the vassal claims that the expenses for the garrison were too great since fewer guards were necessary to garrison the castle, then the expenses are to be paid in accordance with the ruling of an arbiter who will investigate and determine the castle's size or if the lord or vassal were considered enemies at the time. In this way, it will be determined how many guards were necessary to garrison the castle. Indeed, the custom of the land concerning the daily amount given to a vassal for the feeding of his own men will also be considered. In accordance with this ruling, the expenses will be assessed.[10]

---

[10] An idea of these daily wages can be gleaned from the records of Jaume I's aborted crusade of 1269. In the thirteenth century, the highest military salary went to war engineers and then crossbowmen, the lowest to siege and camp laborers. The normal pay for garrison duty was 14 *sous* a day. With the constant escalation of war and the growing use of mercenary service due to the spread of the Hundred Years' War into Spain, wages for soldiers' pay, equipment, and horses steadily increased in the thirteenth and fourteenth centuries. *CAVC*, 2:291; Socarrats, *Commemorationes*, 95; Kagay, "Army Mobilization," 105; Philippe de Contamine, *War in the Middle Ages*, trans. Michael Jones (New York, 1987; repr. Oxford, 1990), 94–95.

10

How Legal Action is Taken Against a Vassal
Who Commits a Crime Against His Lord

If there were two, three, or more vassals in a castle, each subordinate to the next, and the second or third vassal committed a crime against the overlord or the other men of the castle, the overlord should take legal action by suing through the ranks of the vassals. The overlord will thus summon the vassal who holds the castle directly from him and inform him of the crime of the lower vassal, and, for this reason, demand from this man (his immediate vassal) castle control and the posting of a bond.[11] The vassal must immediately post this bond and inform his own vassal about the crime, for which he will also command him to surrender castle control, post bond, and answer the charges of the overlord because of the crime committed against his lord or the men of the castle by the lower vassal. And this second vassal will inform his own vassal — the one who committed the crime — about this action and will command him to surrender castle control, post bond, and answer the charges of the overlord that were preferred about what this last vassal and malefactor is bound to do. And if this last vassal does not comply (that is, if he does not surrender castle control within ten days counting from the day on which he was formally commanded to do so by his own lord), he will be considered a traitor after these ten days have elapsed. The other vassals are bound to help the overlord force this last vassal to surrender castle control, post bond, and answer the overlord's charges. If the other vassals do not do so, they themselves will be considered traitors.

---

[11] The turning over of castle control by more than one castellan involved all of them in paying the expenses incurred by the lord's garrison. Socarrats, *Commemorationes*, 97.

11

How Legal Action is Taken Against a Tenant of an Emphyteusis Who Commits a Crime

Legal action is taken in the same way against the tenant of an emphyteusis. Thus if an overlord should prefer charges against a lesser tenant of an emphyteusis who committed a crime within his own holding, he should take this action against the first tenant; the first should do so with the second; and the second with the third[12] as mentioned above in regard to the vassal. If the third tenant of the emphyteusis delays in posting bond and answering the charges of the overlord after he is formally called to do so by his immediate lord, the overlord then may order the confiscation of the emphyteusis from the tenant tied directly to him; the first may do so from the second and the second from the third. Each time the malefactor defies this confiscation, the overlord may demand a fine from his own tenant who may then do so from the second tenant, and the second may do so from the third, who should pay the fine for defiance of the confiscation order because he acted contrary to the overlord who preferred charges against him. The lord should maintain this series of confiscation orders until the least of these emphyteusis tenants [the malefactor], oppressed by the payment of this fine and admitting his guilt, posts bond and answers the overlord's charges.[13]

---

[12] The problem of subinfeudation of fiefs and mortgaging of other types of tenures was addressed from the *Corts* of Cervera of 1211, which disallowed the proliferation of such divisions by lords and tenants without the overlord's permission. Socarrats, *Commemorationes*, 124; *CAVC*, I, pt. 1:89.

[13] From the period of Jaume I's great conquests, Catalan custom directed that subvassals should post bond with the overlord in such cases. Even before his reign, an attempt was made, in Catalan assemblies of 1202 and 1210, to stop feudal land from being mortgaged, thus starting the process which would eventually turn fiefs into allods. Socarrats, *Commemorationes*, 105, 124; *CAVC*, I, pt. 1:86–87; *Marca hispanica*, 1396–97, doc. 496.

12

Concerning the Commission of a Crime Against the Lord By Other Inhabitants of the Castle

If a lesser castellan takes charge of all the bonds of the legal suits or disputes between the men living in the castle over which he is castellan, or of the inhabitants of any other castle or if the castellan's own retainers commit a crime against or causes any damage to the overlord, his bailiff, or any of the lord's retainers, this malefactor, according to the custom of Catalonia, must post bond, and answer legal charges under the authority of the overlord, and not under that of the castellan — as with a vassal who had committed some crime against his lord.

13

Concerning a Castellan's Allodial Property

If a castellan or vassal claims that he has allodial property within the castle boundary, he must legally prove to his lord that he holds it as a freehold. Since anyone can possess a freehold which originates from a grant or a sale from his lord or from some other freeholder or comes about in some other way, he is not bound to respond legally either in or out of court about this property under the authority of his lord, if he can prove the freehold is his. But if he cannot prove his ownership, the property will be considered not a freehold, but a fief. A prescriptive claim of any time period cannot aid his case, since everything which a castellan or vassal has in the castle boundary is legally included within the fief,[14] unless the contrary can be proven in the above-mentioned way. Thus, the vassal in this case cannot use a prescriptive claim against his lord.

---

[14] The Catalan legists Guillem de Vallseca and Bertran de Seva agreed that one could possess land "separated from the jurisdiction of a castle" which was yet located within the boundary. Socarrats, *Commemorationes*, 140.

14

In Which Cases a Castellan Can Use a Prescriptive Claim Against His Lord and In Which He Cannot[15]

A vassal or castellan can never use a prescriptive claim to justify the refusal to surrender castle control or to render fief service even if he had never rendered service for this fief or if it might be claimed that never in human memory had any of the vassals ever rendered such service or surrendered castle control. However or whenever these duties were carried out or performed, it is sufficient that they were demanded by a lord and that the person they were claimed from was a castellan or vassal, or that he was holding the post of a castellan without being a vassal.

An interpretation of this passage is that a guardian or protector of any underage vassal must do everything demanded by the lord as if he himself really were the lord's vassal until the ward comes of age. In a similar way, castle control should be surrendered by a wife if the vassal is dead. This should be certified by means of a public document; for since it was the same as if this control was demanded from the vassal himself, the public document will show how this surrender of control was carried out and from whom it was surrendered. Thus no prescriptive claim of any length of time may legally aid a vassal in these matters, but instead it favors the lord who makes these demands. Thus the vassal must surrender control of the castle and render service for the fief.

Likewise, if there were sure feudal agreements between a lord and a castellan, in which the lord retains, according to the letter of the pact itself, any lordships, judicial revenues, hospitality, dues, bonds, or anything else, and if over the passage of time a castellan may have received any of these things or anything else that is not contained in the feudal agreement made between the parties, and if the castellan cannot prove that he has title to these things except from the lord's grant, he cannot put forward a prescriptive claim for any length of time, as is obvious from the

---

[15] Socarrats defined the following maxims from this article: "Control over a castle cannot be prescribed even if it was never before surrendered" and "Service done for a fief cannot be prescribed even if it was never performed." This castle or fief service was not unlimited, however, and such scholars as Thomas Mieres declared that once these customary limits were passed, vassals had to be paid, especially for military service. Socarrats, *Commemorationes*, 143–45.

feudal agreement, especially if it is divided with letters of the alphabet.[16] It might be presumed that the castellan had the feudal agreement in his possession, since the lord would have to prove his own case by his copy of the feudal agreement divided by the letters of the alphabet. For in opposition to clear evidence, no long duration of possession should exclude what is owed to the lord. Thus, in an aggregate case (namely, when there were sure agreements between them), no prescriptive claim of any time period can help the castellan's case in refusal to render war service, to carry out military aid owed by the lord's vassals, or to perform certain other duties demanded from vassals in such a castle (in which the lord retained for himself a part of the revenues) except when the feudal agreement established that such revenues were granted by the lord to the castellan's jurisdiction.

---

[16] Such duplicate copies or chirographs guaranteed that the two parties to a contract or agreement had an identical text: M. T. Clanchy, *From Memory to Written Record: England 1066–1307* (London, 1979; repr. London, 1995), 87–88.

15

In What Cases a Castellan Can and Cannot Use a Prescriptive Right Against His Lord

Yet, if a lord does not have a feudal agreement and the castellan does not claim that he and his successors have held and possessed the castle for a period of forty years or more, and it is recognized that he has held it as a fief for his lord, and thus that everything in it belongs to the fief, then a prescriptive claim might favor his case. The only exception is the war service from the type of castle in which the lord retains part of the revenues, the extorted services, the arbitrary tributes, and the military service of the lord's other vassals. Yet, in those matters which might lead to the castle's destruction, the castellan cannot use a prescriptive claim, just as he cannot act to alienate castle properties without his lord's consent. Moreover, a castellan or vassal can never make war from such a castle simply because he has control of it, nor can he impose arbitrary exactions on the inhabitants of the castle nor demand military aids.[17] from those living outside the castle boundaries unless he was given permission to do so by his lord — and this is found to happen very infrequently. Since a castellan must not and cannot lessen the value of his fief for his lord, a prescriptive claim (as mentioned above) does not favor him in these matters, even if none of the lord's predecessors ever made war and extorted arbitrary revenues there. Nevertheless, if this castellan or vassal was pursued by his enemies within the castle boundaries, the men of the castle are required to help him within these limits, but do not have to chase his enemies outside these boundaries. And if these enemies make off with any of the property of the vassal or that of the castle population, the men of the castle can chase the intruders outside the boundaries to retrieve for their lord the things plundered from him, since this booty was stolen from within the castle limits. From this it is not to be interpreted that the men of the castle had been used in war, or had rendered any military aid to the castellan.

---

[17] The *valentia* was a form of military aid that a vassal or castellan swore to give to his lord along with "fealty, help, and good faith." The extent of these aids and the possibility of their exaction was such an unsettled issue that, even during the French invasion of Catalonia of 1284–1285, an embattled Catalan sovereign, Pere II, had to sue his vassal Roger de Luria to try to use aids from castles in peaceful zones to defend northern Catalonia Socarrats, *Commemorationes*, 162, 166; *Marca hispanica*, 1387, doc. 489.

16

That Freeholders Are Bound to Defend a Castle
As Are the Castle Inhabitants Who Possess a Freehold In It

Indeed if any freeholder — whether knight, peasant, or any other person — lives within the boundaries of any castle and there possesses farms, houses, or fortifications (with or without vassals), all of which are freeholds, he, and all other freeholders and all vassals which they have there, must defend the castle and its lord. Vassals who live within the castle boundary as well as the castle lord must defend these freeholders who live in the castle. In wartime, such freeholders must take precautions so their houses or fortresses, which are freeholds, should not cause, or even have the possibility of causing, any damage to the lord and castle inhabitants. But if the lord and castle inhabitants have a clear suspicion that, during wartime, the freeholder had not to the best of his ability offered protection to them, and, as a result, the castle suffered some damage, the freeholder has to surrender the house or fortress to the lord who may keep it as long as the war lasts. All freeholders and all other inhabitants of the castle, except rural freeholders who live outside it, must take part in the following activities: laying ambushes, building siege works, digging trenches, and other things that are necessary for castle defense during wartime.[18]

---

[18] According to Socarrats, the castle consisted of "walls and inhabitants." Several suits, including one decided by Socarrats himself in 1387, upheld the right of a castle lord or castellan to claim such work, even from the freeholders living with the castle complex. Socarrats, *Commemorationes*, 170, 175–76.

17

Under Whose Authority Freeholders Must File Suit

If a freeholder lives in any castle, and the castle lord sues him, claiming that his property was not allodial, the freeholder does not have to file suit in the castle lord's tribunal, but both must come under the control of a mutually acceptable party who will resolve their dispute. If they cannot agree on a mutually acceptable party, if, for example, the person whom the freeholder chooses does not suit the castle lord, and the freeholder wants to submit to the authority of the ruler or his vicar, the castle lord, willing or not, must accept and may not withdraw from the suit, since the ruler or his vicar stand as a common party for all inhabitants in this land. Yet if there is a dispute between the freeholder and any other vassal of the castle lord, the freeholder does not have to post bond under the castle lord's authority if this was the ancient custom. Yet, in this case, the castle lord can successfully make a prescriptive claim against such freeholders. But if no such custom exists, the above-mentioned case should be carried out as follows: the freeholder still must post bond with the lord of the castle where the freehold is located if he owns other properties in this castle; this also applies if, in line with custom, he has filed other types of suits there — that is, those involving debt or assault — with castle inhabitants.

18

When a Castellan Can and Cannot Transfer
a Part of the Castle Without the Consent of His Lord

Without his lord's consent, a castellan or feudatory cannot transfer ownership of his castle or fief, nor any part of them in which the lord receives part of the castle or fief revenues by any type of transfer. But if the castle were to be such that the lord receives none of the castle revenues, but only castle control, or, if the fief is not a castle or fortress but rather another type of property, such as fields, vineyards, revenues, or the like that has no castle of any kind attached for which control is either demanded or given, but only requires that an oath of homage be taken and some service rendered during wartime or during general hosts: in this case, such a vassal can without his lord's consent establish in perpetuity any part of his fief as an emphyteusis. This is so since such an arrangement must result in the increase, and not the decrease, of the fief's value, for in such an transfer the fief's value is not lessened; nor does the lord lose anything, because he traditionally received none of the castle or fief revenues.[19] Besides, that part of the fief which was designated as an emphyteusis by the vassal remains under the lord's authority, and is not separated from the fief. In fact, no one, neither the lord nor the vassal, should retain authority in such an transfer. Even though a vassal of this type will surrender full control of his castle, he must render homage and perform full service to his lord for the fief, as his predecessors formerly did, even if he established none of his fief as an emphyteusis. There are other types of transfers, such as donations, sales etc., in which no lordship is retained.[20] The vassal cannot retain any of these types without the lord's permission, since even though the lord receives none of the revenues, the vassal cannot diminish the fief for his lord.

---

[19] Socarrats declared that the custom of Barcelona allowed the subdivision of a fief and proclaimed that each subdivision constituted an alienation. According to the *Libri Feudorum*, a vassal could alienate one-half of his fief without his lord's consent. Socarrats, *Commemorationes*, 213; *Libri Feudorum*, 500, bk. I, tit. 13.

[20] Socarrats asserted that only the alienation of a castle involved control; a fief involved no such transfer, but only "just homage." In a sense, then, this differentiation between a holding which could be ceded to another and that which could not probed the meanings of the Roman legal terms "jurisdiction" (*ius; iurisdictio*), "dominion" (*imperium*), and "power, ownership" (*dominium*). Pere Albert raises a similar question in article 36. Socarrats, *Commemorationes*, 189; Pennington, *Prince and the Law*, 102–3; Berman, *Law and Revolution*, 289–91; Brian Tierney, *The Idea of Natural Rights: Studies on Natural Rights, Natural Law, and Church Law, 1150–1625* (Atlanta, GA, 1996), 30–42.

19

Whether a Lord Can Lessen a Fief or Remove a Vassal from a Fief

If a lord wishes to sell any castle of his for which he has a vassal who is a knight, he must take into consideration the rank of the person to whom the castle is to be sold; for if the buyer is a townsman, villager, or peasant, the vassal who is a knight is not obliged to render service or post bond for such a buyer or engage in litigation for the fief. The same applies to other minor fiefs. If the fief is sold to a church, the vassal is bound to render homage to whichever prelate the church designates. If, however, the castle is sold to a knight, care must be taken that the purchaser should be of as low a rank as the vassal and the vassal of as noble a rank as the purchaser, since the vassal cannot hold the fief from one of a lower rank without bringing dishonor on himself. Thus, for instance, if the vassal is a count or viscount who is invested with some great fief because of his lineage, as well as the greatness of his lordship, then such a vassal is not bound to render homage to the buyer who is a knight of a lower rank. But, if the vassal can hold the fief without undergoing any dishonor from the knightly buyer, even though he is of a lesser rank and lineage than the lord who sold it, the vassal must render homage to the knightly buyer. Yet some say that a lord cannot reduce the rank of the vassal's lord, just as the vassal cannot reduce the rank of the lord's vassal. But this is not true, since a vassal without the consent of his lord cannot sell the fief, but a lord, without the consent of his vassal, can sell it to whomever he wishes, even over the objection of his vassal. Besides, if the lord has given him permission to do so, the vassal has to sell the fief to a man of equal rank. Otherwise, he cannot sell it to a man of lesser rank except with his lord's permission. The same applies to emphyteusis tenants and other feudatories.

20

How the Buyer of a Castle Is to Be Placed in Possession of It

If a castle or fief in which there are one or more vassals is sold and the lordly seller wishes to establish a buyer in possession of it, he will gather both peasants and other men before him and the buyer at the church or at some other site in the castle. In the presence of the buyer, the selling lord will call out the name of each of the vassals and they, rising, should come before the seller and buyer. The lordly seller, announcing the sale before them all, should absolve them from every oath of homage and fealty to him, so that from then on none of these peasants is under his obligation for anything in this castle or fief. He will then command them to render homage to the buyer as their lord; they each must immediately do this in the customary way. The seller will then order the peasants and other inhabitants of the castle to do the same thing. If there is a large group of them, three, four or a greater number of the more important inhabitants, chosen with the consent of the buyer, should render homage to the new lord on behalf of themselves and all the others.[21] Afterwards, the lordly seller should station the buyer on a castle dwelling, or any other house if there is no such structure in the castle. He should approve of the buyer's rights in this way: "Therefore I place you in possession of this castle."[22] The buyer should have a banquet prepared there, and after the meal is over, the seller may depart if he wishes to.

---

[21] This group homage was similar to the large meetings of Aragonese nobles and townsmen (dating from at least the eleventh century) who rendered homage to the monarch at the beginning of his reign. Bisson, "Problem of Feudal Monarchy," 465–66.

[22] This is obviously a standardized notarial form in which the names of the seller and buyer would be inserted when needed. The same type of forms for the recording of a fealty oath were used from the reign of Ramon Berenguer III. *Usatges*, trans. Kagay, 120; Trenchs Odena, "La escribanía de Ramón Berenguer III," 36.

21

When a Lord's Choice Comes into Play in
the Grant of a Fief to the Son of a Deceased Vassal

If a vassal dies intestate and leaves two, three, or more sons, born from a legitimate marriage, this is a situation for a lordly choice.[23] According to the gloss,[24] this choice should come into play when no permissible and obligatory legal provisions have been established between lord and vassal for the situation after the latter's death. When such provisions have been stipulated, they must be observed . . .[25] since the lord can grant the fief to any of the sons he wishes and invest him with the fief, after receiving homage from him. He can do this even if the other sons are opposed to this action. Whether the other brothers file suit over the fief or not, it will legally remain in the possession of the heir.

---

[23] *Gratificatio*, according to Socarrats, was defined "as the designation of which heir was to serve in a fief." Jaume de Callis asserted that this lordly prerogative originated in the "ancient times" of the Spanish March before there were fiefs and when the Catalan counts only had such retainers as "viscounts, vasvassores, *comitores* and knights." Socarrats, *Commemorationes*, 221.

[24] *Glossa* here refers to the explanation of a difficult word or concept appended to the manuscript versio of the *Commemorationes* which Socarrats retained in his first printed text of the work. For glosses and glossators of Roman and canon law texts, see Bellomo, *Common Legal Past of Europe*, 129–33; R. H. Helmholtz, *The Spirit of Classical Canon Law* (Athens, GA, 1996), 15–17.

[25] For better meaning, I have deleted the following words, "as, for example, in the pasturage of a hundred good cows and in the *Usatges*, (trans. Kagay, 71, art. 27) concerning the fiefs of the intestate 'If anyone, from viscount . . .'."

22

How Control Must Be Surrendered by a Woman
Who Succeeds to a Fief

In accordance with the general usage and observance of Catalonia, if a deceased castellan or vassal is survived by a daughter, she succeeds to the fief just as a male offspring does. If the daughter is a minor ward, her guardian in her stead should then render homage, surrender castle control whenever requested, render service, and post bond for the fief to the lord of the fief. If he should act contrary to what fealty requires, he will be considered a traitor.[26] The guardian will thus remain the heir's vassal as long as his guardianship lasts. But if the lady should marry, her husband must surrender castle control and render all services as a vassal if he received this fief as part of a dowry. He cannot refuse to carry out these services, since by a legal fiction he is considered the lord. Therefore, if he does not render homage and surrender castle control, or does anything contrary to what fealty requires, he will be considered a traitor. But if castle control was demanded not from the husband, but from the lady herself, and the lady does not surrender control, the lord of the castle must because of this return this castle to the husband. Yet if the fief was not given in the dowry, but was included in the lady's personal possessions,[27] then the said lady, and not her husband, should render homage to the lord, either in person or by a representative, as she wishes. In the same way, she should give castle control and do everything that fealty requires in regard to this fief.

---

[26] José María Lalinde Abadia, "Los pactos matrinoniales catalanes," *AHDE* 33 (1963): 251–52, doc. 5. For similar practice in contemporary Champagne, see Evergates, trans., *Feudal Society*, 51–52, doc. 35.

[27] *Paraphernalia* was personal property of the wife not included in the dowry. Socarrats, *Commemorationes*, 237.

23

That a Vassal Cannot Abandon a Fief to the Lord

After a vassal renders homage to his lord for any fief, and the lord, upon receiving this homage and fealty, grants the fief to him, the feudatory cannot desert his lord nor abandon the fief without his lord's consent. Indeed, he must retain the fief and remain the lord's vassal. The same applies if an heir of this type, at his father's death, accedes to his fief, since, in this case, a person cannot refuse homage to a lord for fiefs. Even if unwilling to do so, the son thus must retain the fief as a vassal and be compelled to render homage to the lord. According to the gloss, this is so because the same person represents the deceased father in the fief, and thus if the deceased father could not evade his legal responsibilities by abandoning the fief, then neither can the son evade the responsibilities of homage, after he has acceded to a feudal holding.[28] But if he had not acceded to it, he may not be compelled to retain the fief.[29]

---

[28] Socarrats draws a distinction between a vassal's purposeful abandonment of a fief and the loss of such holdings due to vassalic treason or some other crime. In such cases, as with Jaume III of Majorca in 1343, the treasonous lord, not only lost his feudal holdings, but his vassals also had to aid the overlord in recovering these lands. Socarrats, *Commemorationes*, 248–49; Pere III, *Crònica*, trans. Hillgarth, 1:303–8, bk. III, chaps. 71–83.

[29] Compare with the more fluid situation in medieval Champagne in which a vassal could resign his fief to take service with a wealthier or more generous lord and then reclaim it, alleging he had acted from "evil advice." Evergates, trans., *Feudal Society*, 54, 75, docs. 37, 55(A), 55(B).

24

Whether Either a Possessor of a Usufruct or a Tenant is Bound to Render Homage or Service[30]

If a vassal or castellan bequeaths to his son a castellany[31] or a castle fief, retaining for himself only the use of it for the rest of his life but then if the lord demands that he render homage to him; and, in the meantime, if his son claims that he and not his father should be the principal vassal from whom homage should be demanded, since his father had only retained use of the castle and had settled the title of principal vassal on him in this fief from the time of his accession to the grant which his father made to him; and further if the father and usufructuary feared that he would lose use of the castle if the son, the principal vassal, rendered homage to the lord, and then if the same father objected and claimed that he, and not his son, should render homage: in this case, after each of these parties has offered himself as vassal, the lord can receive homage from each — from the father as usufructuary and from the son as a principal vassal. The exceptions to this are that the usufructuary should always retain his status, and that the lord should receive service only from this usufructuary. Thus there are not two, but only one vassal for this fief, and because of this the lord should issue an official document for this fief, so that this arrangement should not be legally prejudiced in any way. According to the gloss, if the castellan retained nothing for himself at the time of the inheritance or grant, but rather bequeathed all of his castellany or fief to his son, then the son — if his father had fully bequeathed these things to him while retaining nothing for himself — is bound to render homage to the lord of the castle or fief, after he has acceded to the fief which his father had bestowed on him in this way. But if the son refuses to render homage, and the lord of the castle or fief, because of this, confiscates the holding and retains it through armed force, he

---

[30] The issue of splitting the castellany and determining which party owed fealty, homage and service came up in a number of fourteenth-century suits, the most important of which involved Catalan clergy who used clerical agents to hold castles, as well as the count of Barcelona who was reminded that no lord, not even the prince, could "continually hold fortresses and castles." Socarrats, *Commemorationes*, 255.

[31] The "castellany" (*castlania*) consisted of a complex of privileges and revenues attached to a castle that were normally controlled by a castellan. Pierre Bonnassie, *La Catalogne du milieu du Xᵉ à la fin du XIᵉ siècle: Croissance et mutation d'une sociéte*, 2 vols. (Toulouse, 1975–1976), 2:751–54.

is not obliged to return the castle or fief until the son renders homage to him and reimburses him for all the expenses and damages that he can prove occurred and that he suffered from the day on which the son had refused to render homage until that on which the matter was settled.

25

When Two Castellans Hold Just One Castle for a Lord and They Do Not Alternate in Holding the Castellany

If there were two castellans in any castle and one of them did not hold the castellany for the other, but instead they, one after the other in succession, hold the castellany for a third person (their lord), then one of them should take control of all the bonds while the other keeps none of them. If any of the inhabitants of this castle commit a crime against the castellan who does not retain the bonds or against the overlord, these malefactors, according to the custom of Catalonia, are bound to post bond and answer legal charges for their crime under the jurisdiction of the castellan who generally receives and holds the bonds from the other inhabitants of the castle.

26

When a Vassal is Bound to Render Homage to His Lord's Successor

Normally, if the successor of one's deceased lord demands it from him, a vassal must immediately render homage to him [the successor]. It does not favor the vassal's argument if, in opposition, he claims that neither he nor his ancestors ever rendered homage to the lord who was now deceased, or his ancestors; or that it was not specified in the legal instrument by which the fief was granted that homage had to be rendered in exchange for it. The vassal is not aided in a complaint against rendering homage by the above-mentioned arguments, because, in this case, it is clear that he is a vassal, and when the lord demands homage for this fief, the vassal must render it to him.

27

If a Person Can Be Considered Guilty of Treason Before He Renders Homage

If a vassal or a castellan or his successor commits the crime of treason against his lord before he swears homage and fealty for his fief to the lord or his successor, the vassal must be judged a traitor if he or his successor acceded as an heir to the fief by a last will or grant and then stood in service to the lord of this fief against whom the treason was committed.

28

When and In Which Cases Homage Must Be Renewed

Within a year and a day[32] of his lord's death, the vassal must come before the deceased lord's heir to renew homage and swear fealty to him. If he does not so within the stated period, he will be considered contumacious,[33] and as such may lose his fief if the lord is in favor of it. Similarly, with the death of a vassal and the accession of his heir — whoever that might be — to the inheritance, the successor must come before the lord of the fief within the stated period after the death of his predecessor. Prepared to render homage and swear fealty, he should demand to be invested with the fief. Yet, once he accedes to this inheritance, he must be linked to the lord by an oath of fealty and an act of homage. But if he neglects to carry out these things, he should lose his fief, if the lord is in favor of it. But if in these two cases the lord does not want the vassal or his heir to lose the fief, he can sue him or his heir to force the recognition of his lordship by carrying out the aforesaid measures — not so the heir may be punished for his contumacy, but because he acceded to immunitary land[34] against his lord's consent. Thus it is the usage and observance [of Catalonia] that once an heir has acceded to his inheritance, he represents the deceased person, from whom he had inherited these holdings.

---

[32] Compare with succession norms established in the twelfth-century *Libri Feudorum*, 498–506, bk. 1, tit. viii, nos. 1, 3; tit. xxii, xxvi.

[33] *Contumacia* consisted of failure to carry out orders or duties imposed by a superior authority, whether a feudal lord, a prince, or a court.

[34] The *immunitas* was land, like the fief, which was exempt from royal justice and jurisdiction.

29

Concerning the Penalty for a Vassal Who Refuses to Render Service to a Lord That He is Bound to Carry Out

If a castellan or vassal unjustly refuses to render service to his lord (as he must do to the fullest of his ability in accordance with the feudal pact) and, because of this, the lord confiscates his fief, then, in such a case, he is not obliged to return the fief to the vassal until the value of the service is reimbursed twice over. From then on, the vassal must not refuse service and has to fully assure the lord through bonds that he will carry it out. In such a case, the lord should confiscate the revenues attached to the fief, as long as he controls it. He will keep the confiscated fief until the vassal has certified under bond that, because of his own default, his lord was within his rights.

30

Concerning Different Kinds of Homage

There are two types of homage[35] namely, liege homage and non-liege homage. Liege homage is that which involves a type of rendering of homage and fealty. Thus the liege vassal renders fealty to his lord against all others, and no one is exempted from this last group, whether by oral agreement or by the correct understanding of the terms. The person who holds a general jurisdiction is considered to be exempt, and therefore the liege vassal is not obliged to aid his lord against a person holding such an exemption.[36] From this it is clear that no one is understood to be exempt, except when he possesses a general jurisdiction. Thus no one can render liege homage to two lords.

However, homage is non-liege when one provides an exception when rendering homage by saying to his lord the following: "I render homage to you with this one exception: namely, that I may commend myself to some other man against whom I do not wish to be bound to aid you." Yet if a specific exception is not granted, the same thing is accomplished if the following words are uttered: "In rendering this homage, I am a non-liege vassal, since I am not bound to render fealty against all men." Indeed, the vassal may exclude persons against whom he does not have to render homage or give help.

---

[35] Socarrats, following Jaume Marquilles, claimed that homage did not originate with Roman or Visigothic law, "but from usages and customs." Socarrats, *Commemorationes*, 309.

[36] This "general jurisdiction" (*generalis jurisdictio*) is similar to "public utility" (*publica utilitas*) discussed in article 39. These terms often applied to the Catalan sovereign, the count of Barcelona, but did not always have to.

31

To Whom a Lord's Liege Vassal Can Render Homage and to Whom He Cannot

A liege vassal of any noble must not and cannot render homage to his lord's enemy if his lord is unwilling or has not even been consulted. Yet in non-liege homage, fealty which a vassal owes to his liege lord always contains exceptions. But if the lord to whom he renders non-liege homage is not his original lord's enemy, and if, when consulted, he did not oppose it, then the liege vassal of this lord can render [non-liege] homage to the second lord. In this case, the lord's prohibition must be observed by his liege vassal.[37]

---

[37] Compare with Jaime II's law of 1292: "No man who has a farm, plot of land, or anything else with the lordship of another person ... can take a vassal for this property without the lord's consent." Socarrats, *Commemorationes*, 314.

32

How a Liege Vassal of Two Lords is to Conduct Himself When These Lords Wage War on Each Other

If a person is a liege vassal of two lords for two different fiefs, and it happens that these two lords wage war against each other, the vassal is bound to aid the lord to whom he first rendered homage. Thus he must serve the first lord and is understood to be exempt from service to the second. According to custom, he is not bound to aid the second lord to whom he rendered homage, except out of kindness and a certain sense of impartiality. Therefore he should aid the first lord to whom he rendered homage and may help the second with a substitute since such matters can be disposed of equitably through a substitute. In doing this, he will comply with the terms of the fealty that he promised to his second lord — that is, that he would help him alone and would help no one against him, with the exception of his first liege lord — since he does not seem to render aid against his first lord, even though he had provided help to the second through an alternate. This action was not taken to harm the first lord, but was carried out by the vassal in an attempt to protect his own position and not to lose the fief given him by the second lord. If any doubt arises concerning which of the lords he was primarily bound to render personal aid to from the terms of the homage (for instance, because his ancestors had begun to render homage in the distant past, and from the terms of the homage it was not obvious which of the two lords had the previous feudal claim over the vassal), the vassal can thus impartially give his personal aid to whichever of the two lords he chooses, provided he serves the other with a substitute. Yet as is stated above, he should not do this with the intention of causing harm.[38]

---

[38] The question of a liege vassal caught between two warring liege lords caused considerable disagreement among Catalan legists in the century before Socarrats's commentary. The majority followed this schema of the vassal fighting for one lord and providing a substitute for the other. One, Guillem the Provost, cited a case of 1396, in which a vassal attempting this tactic was fined for violating his oath of homage to one of his lords. Socarrats, *Commemorationes*, 312.

33

How a Freeman Can Establish Himself as Another's Vassal and Render Homage to Him. What is Involved in Rendering Homage and When It Should Be Initiated

Although according to Roman law a free man cannot become the slave of another by any kind of simple petition, or even by a legal grant, nevertheless one can lessen his status by decree.[39] Thus, by putting the petition in writing, any free man can establish himself as the vassal of any lord and can render homage to him. As stated in the feudal pact, the ceremony is carried out according to the general custom of Catalonia in the following way: the lord must hold between his hands the hands of the person rendering homage. Kneeling, the vassal renders homage according to the terms of the feudal pact, promising fealty with his hands in between his lord's hands.[40] As a sign that the lord will be faithful to him, he

---

[39] The proclaimed *raison d'être* of the *Usatges* was to fill the gaps of Roman and Visigothic law for the society of twelfth-century Catalonia. One of the most difficult problems of the new code was the adaptation of the workings of feudalism into the thought-world of Roman jurisprudence. Roman jurists drew the clear distinction between those who exercised jurisdiction over themselves (freemen) and those under the jurisdiction of others (slaves). A freeman had the right to alter his status before the law by being adopted by an older man or entering into a work contract. An individual was not free to engage in status-loss from freedom; this could take place only as the result of a criminal verdict which decreed loss of citizenship and transferral to slavery. Some few exceptions to this are seen in Justinian's *Novels*. By Visigothic times, the barrier between free and slave no longer remained as absolute for freemen, either willing or not, who could be sold into slavery and see their children branded with this servile status. *The Digest of Justinian*, trans. Alan Watson, 2 vols. (Philadelphia, 1998), I.6.1, 7.1–2; *Justinian's Institutes*, trans. Peter Birks and Grant McLeod (Ithaca, NY, 1987), 49, 1.16.1; *Leges Visigothorum*. Monumenta Germaniae Historica. Legum: sectio I, ed. Karl Zeumer (Hanover, 1902), 221, 5.4.11; *Usatges*, trans. Kagay, 63, chap. 2; J. A. Crook, *Law and Life of Rome, 90B.C.–A.D. 212* (Ithaca, NY, 1967), 196; Roger Bagnall, "Slavery and Society in Late Roman Egypt," in *Law, Politics, and Slavery in the Ancient Mediterranean World*, ed. B. Halpern and D. Hobson (Sheffield, 1993), 220–40; P. D. King, *Law and Society in the Visigothic Kingdom* (Cambridge, 1972), 75, 90–91, 159–78.

[40] For other oaths of homage including that of Galbert of Bruges, see *History of Feudalism*, ed. Herlihy, 98–101, docs. 15–16. Compare with the general oath described in the *Libri Feudorum*: "Titius, swear on these four Gospels that from this hour I will be faithful to you, lord Caius, as my lord against all men except the emperor or the king." *Libri Feudorum*, 511, bk. II, tit. vii.

kisses his vassal. Indeed, the lord owes the same kind of allegiance to his vassal as the vassal owes his lord. The vassal will be obliged to help and protect the lord from his enemies to the best of his ability within his jurisdiction. Even though homage is not set down in writing according to Roman civil law,[41] nevertheless this practice is established by a long-standing usage of Catalonia — which is similar to a law. Therefore, this usage is supported and defended by Roman law: since valid agreements must be observed.[42]

---

[41] Even Roman law clearly defined a slave as one made captive during war or born to a slave mother, a form of limited civil status often attached to a freedman who remained under the "statutory guardianship" (*legitima tutela*) of his former master or "patron" (*patronus*). From this type of legally-recognized dependence under Roman law, the many types of feudal relations would emerge, but only after Rome had been replaced by the barbarian kingdoms. *Digest of Justian*, trans. Watson, 1.5.5; *Justianian's Intitutes*, trans. Birks and McLeod, 49, 1.17; Barbero and Vigil, *Formación del feudalismo*, 21–52.

[42] For discussion of honoring contracts in Roman law, see *Justinian's Institutes*, trans. Birks and McLeod, 105–7; 3.3.13–14, Crook, *Law and Life of Rome*, 214–15.

34

Whether a Prescriptive Claim Can Be Made For Homage and How Homage Is Attained

A prescriptive claim can be made for homage if any noble has not received service from another, whether liege vassal or peasant, in the past thirty years. After this period the noble is barred from claiming homage; similarly, after this same period of thirty years the act of homage cannot bind the noble. Yet after ten or twenty years if anyone as liege vassal withholds his service to a noble on the grounds of a prescriptive claim, even though he had rendered such services during this period, and then denies that he is his lord's liege vassal, then the noble himself has an excuse for taking matters into his own hands by saying the following: "Boy, you are my vassal; by feudal pact, you have promised to render service to me unless the terms of another homage should intervene." Thus, with the passage of time, the claim [to homage] is presumed to be in effect.

Nevertheless, a noble who makes such a claim must be careful not to violate the oath of frivolous litigation.[43] Yet, it must be diligently observed that a freeman cannot assert exemption by prescriptive claim after a term of a ten, twenty, thirty, or even forty years, since such a prescriptive limit has no place in the homage of freemen except from the type of previous legal title discussed above. Therefore it is crystal clear that homage is attained in two ways: namely, by prescription or by agreement. It is attained by prescription after the long period of thirty or forty years. This is true if during this time, one receives from another services similar to those rendered to a lord. Yet, if he receives service from another (as from a friend), no prescriptive claim applies. A prescriptive claim can be made by promise on the basis of a charter or a feudal pact. According to custom, in the making of [homage by] agreement, it is not important if a legal claim was in place on not for even though a claim has not been filed, yet the agreement is valid with the application of the feudal pact. A claim is also in effect when the following is stated in the agreement: "Therefore I establish myself as your vassal, since you have given me such and such a fief, so you must defend me in my jurisdiction from so and so, my enemies, or as a punishment for the crimes you say I have committed against you."

---

[43] Litigants in the Roman system had to swear that they were forced to file suit on good legal grounds and not through any abuse of "court procedure." In early Republican law, litigants guilty of "frivolous litigation" (*calumnia*) would forfeit one-tenth of their claim. *Justinian's Institutes*, trans. Birks and McLeod, 143, 4.16.1.

35

Whether the Son of a Vassal Might or Might Not Be the Vassal of His Father's Lord

When considering whether or how homage has been established, it must be understood if a vassal's son, himself, may be feudally tied to his father's lord. In this situation, it must be determined who rendered homage and when he did so. In this case, the son of the person who rendered simple homage is not a vassal of the lord since homage has already been rendered [by his father]. In this matter, it must also be determined whether homage has been rendered to redress a crime against another (for instance, if he had killed the father of the person to whom he rendered homage) or since he has sworn homage only to maintain peaceful relations whether he is truly a vassal to the one to whom he swore homage.

The long-approved custom is that a son must not suffer for the crime of his father, and thus it is true that, if the son renders simple homage in redress for this crime, he does not subordinate his own property as a fief to the person to whom he renders the homage. It is different, however, in the case of a person who, when rendering homage, surrenders his property and then receives it back from his lord as a fief. In this situation, if the sons of the person who had rendered homage do not want to take possession of their father's property, the lord to whom homage had been rendered cannot take vengeance on them through his other vassals. However, if these sons wish to take control of their father's holdings and formally recognize this, it is clear that they are the lord's vassals, since the property, along with the responsibilities attached to it, has been transferred. If the sons wish to take possession of this property, they should render homage to the lord, recognizing the responsibility their father had carried out. According to custom, the person who renders homage becomes the liege vassal of the lord to whom he has promised it. Since this lord gave him something as a fief, in return, he should defend and protect the person of the lord. Because in this case it may be presumed that the father was principally obliged to care for, defend, and protect the person to whom he rendered homage, it may also be presumed that the lord would wish to care for [his vassal's] sons, as he did for their father. Thus in this case it is certain that the persons of the sons are bound by the right of homage and the son of any vassal will be the vassal of the lord to whom their father rendered homage.

As we have mentioned, this is the custom of France and of many other places and regions. But in Catalonia it is not the custom, and in fact this matter is carried out differently. For when anyone, whether a knight or a peasant, establishes himself as a liege vassal by rendering homage to any magnate, the lord should give some kind of fief or the equivalent to him. If the person who renders homage is a knight, vassals of this magnate's new man are not bound to render homage to him, except when his son or sons accede to the inheritance of their father. This is how things are done throughout Catalonia. But if the person who renders homage is a peasant, the custom is observed differently, since in a certain part of Catalonia called Old Catalonia[44] (as well as in all of the bishopric of Barcelona which is beyond the Llobregat River toward the east and in the majority of the bishopric of Vich) serfs,[45] who are not knights, are thus bound to their lords, and their sons are the vassals of their lords. Thus, they can neither contract marriage nor leave the estate. But if they do so, the lord can take legal actions to bring them back. If they contract marriage, the lords of these peasants can take a fourth of the dowry. Yet if the sons of these peasants or the peasants themselves leave without the permission of the lords of their holdings and afterwards take up residence in the villages of the sovereign, churchmen, or other nobles of Catalonia for a year and a day, and if they have not been forbidden to live in these places by their lords or they themselves are unwilling to redeem themselves from their lords, they can remain there safe and sound after the year and a day have elapsed, in accordance with the ancient and long-approved custom of Catalonia; neither knights nor churchmen can claim them back.

Yet in another part of Catalonia (which is across the aforesaid Llobregat River, and which from the time of the lord king [Ramon] Berenguer [IV] and afterwards has been called New Catalonia), neither the sons of knights nor those of peasants are vassals of those magnates to whom their fathers were vassals unless, as stated above, they have acceded to the feudal holding. Likewise, all the serfs who are peasants can leave the land whenever they want to, and so can their sons, after renouncing their feudal holdings, but they must always remain the vassals of their lords, and may be compelled to render homage as it has been described above.

---

[44] Socarrats cites a number of examples from Old Catalonia [Gerona, San Baudilio, and the monastery of Sant Cugat] to show that the custom was that "the vassal of another was bound to take an oath of fealty and homage to the lord of the castle." Socarrats, *Commemorationes*, 347.

[45] Pere Albert and most succeeding Catalan legists of the Middle Ages signified by the term *homines solidi* (when associated with peasants) not liege vassals, but serfs (*homines de remença*) who could win their freedom only by the payment of a sizeable bond. Freedman contends that the term *homines solidi* could refer to free peasants, but by the fifteenth century had come to mean serfs. Freeman, "Origins of Serfdom," 294–99. See also Jaume Vicens Vives, *Història de las remensas (en el sigle XV)* (Barcelona, 1976), 18–31.

36

Whether Anyone Can Be the Liege Vassal of Two Lords and Whether a Woman Can be a Liege Vassal and How She Should Render Homage For Her Fief To Her Lord

According to the custom of Catalonia or even Roman law, no one can be a liege vassal of two lords since, just as two men cannot have ownership of the same thing, thus two men cannot have the right of liege homage over the same vassal. For, according to the custom of Catalonia, with the death of the liege vassal of any noble (for instance, the viscount of Cardona)[46] and the succession of the deceased vassal's daughter to the liege fief that her dead father had held for his lord, the viscount, the daughter will be his vassal. But if it happens that this woman should marry any knight who is the liege vassal of another noble (for instance, the count of Urgel)[47] and should give to her husband (the liege vassal of the count) her own liege fief, she may do so as a necessary provision of the dowry in accordance with the custom of Catalonia. But her husband, the knight, cannot establish himself as a liege vassal of the viscount of Cardona, since he is already a liege vassal of the count of Urgel. Yet, in accordance with the aforesaid custom, this woman who succeeds to the fief will remain the vassal of her lord, and will render homage and fealty to the viscount of Cardona, the lord for whom she held the fief. However, though the custom of Catalonia allows a daughter to accede to the fief, yet she will use an intermediary to give the kiss [of fealty] and serve as a vassal is obliged to. Indeed, since it is not fitting for a woman to bear arms,[48] she

---

[46] One of the great viscomital family that, from the tenth century, came to dominate the counties of the eastern Pyrenees, as well as a number of important towns, including Manresa, Cervera, Berga, Solsona, and Igualada. Santiago Sobrequès i Vidal, *Els barons de Catalunya* (Barcelona, 1957; repr. Barcelona, 1980), 41–45, 100–5.

[47] A Catalan county, south of Pallars bisected by the Segre River, which remained independent from the late tenth century until the death of its last native count, Ermengol VIII, in 1208. The county was fought over by the Cardona and Cabrera families through much of Jaume I's lifetime, but eventually after his death came under the influence of the French count of Foix. Sobrequès, *Barons*, 17–22, 65–58.

[48] For the prohibition of and reality of women bearing arms, see Contamine, *War in the Middle Ages*, 241–42; Jean A. Truax, "Anglo-Norman Women at War: Valiant Soldiers, Prudent Strategists or Charismatic Leaders?" in *The Circle of War in the Middle Ages: Essays on Medieval Military and Naval History*, ed. Donald J. Kagay and L. J. Andrew Villalon (Woodbridge, Suffolk, 1999), 111–25.

should send to her lord one or many armed men in her place if the fief or feudal agreement demands such military service. In this way she can carry out her responsibilities well by another person. But if her husband is not a liege vassal of the count of Urgel or anyone else, he will himself be bound to carry out all these duties for the lord of the fief from whom he received this feudal holding in the dowry. Indeed, if he did not receive such feudal holdings in the dowry, but rather among the non-dowry property, he does not have to perform this service if he is unwilling to do so, and then the wife is bound to do so in the method mentioned above.

37

Whether A Vassal Is Bound to Accompany His Lord to Distant Lands[49]

If any lord greatly wishes to travel to the distant lands of the Saracens to make war against them, he can command his vassals to accompany him if he is the kind of lord strong enough to make war on the Saracens, as are the kings of Aragon, France, Castile, and certain other princes, and his predecessors customarily did so. Such a lord can summon his vassals and others of his subjects skilled in the use of weapons to travel with him to the regions of the Saracens.[50] Yet the king is

---

[49] The question of traveling to far lands with one's lord was connected with the issue of vassalic military service. The *Usatges* opened up the possibility that such service was not unlimited by declaring that there was a customary boundary to a vassal's military duty to his lord and, if this was exceeded, the lord had to pay his salary, or at least reimburse his losses. If the lord wished permanently to increase the level of such service, he had to grant his vassal a larger fief. This means of regulating service largely remained in effect down to 1292 when both equity and custom were established as guides for making such determinations. In the second half of Jaume I's long reign, the vassalic duty of serving on campaigns in Muslim *Hispania* was at the center of more than one baronial bout of resistance. In 1273 Ramón Folç IV, viscount of Cardona, and a group of Catalan barons refused to aid Jaume I in putting down an insurrection of Valencian Muslims before a judge had been appointed to determine if the required service was "according . . . to the *Usatges of Barcelona*." The response of Jaume I and his son Pere II was to label Cardona and his associates as rebels and traitors. Despite the threat of royal action, the question of foreign service for vassals remained a paramount legal issue before royal courts. By the reign of Pere III legists, at least, defined "foreign soil" as anything beyond the Catalan boundaries, even lands of the realms of the Crown of Aragon. Socarrats, *Commemorationes*, 385–86, 390, 395; *CAVC*, 1, pt. 1:159–60, art. 33; *Usatges*, trans. Kagay, 72, arts. 30, 32; Miret i Sans, *Itinerari*, 478; Kagay, "Structures," 62; idem, "*Princeps namque*," 1–32; Manuel Cubells, "Documentos diplomáticos aragoneses (1259–1284)," *Revue Hispanique* 27 (1916): 150–51, docs. 51–52; Sobrequès, *Barons*, 101–2.

[50] From early in the crusading movement, the papacy strictly divided the Saracen enemy Christendom faced between those infidel forces which overran the Holy Land and eastern Mediterranean from those which threatened the Iberian Peninsula and the western Mediterranean. In 1096, shortly after he had preached what would become the First Crusade, Pope Urban II (1088–1099) urged the Spanish to continue their long fight against the Muslims who controlled over half of the peninsula. To Urban, it made no sense to free Asia from "Saracen tyranny" while leaving the Christian realms of Iberia undefended. Whether the long series of wars the Spanish Christians fought against the Muslim realms of

bound to reimburse his vassals totally, or at least partially, if the fiefs that they hold from him are small. This must be determined by the judgement of an arbiter who will take into consideration the size of the fief and whether the journey is a long or a short one. But if the lord is not the type who is strong enough to make war on the Saracens, and his ancestors did not customarily wage war on nor invade the Saracens, neither his own vassals nor their vassals are bound to accompany him to distant lands, even though he can call them out to render such service against his personal enemies against whom he might have a war.

---

the peninsula were true crusades is an academic battle that rages to this very day. José Goñi Gaztambide, *Historia de la bula de la cruzada en España* (Vitoria, 1958), 60–61; Robert I. Burns, "The Many Crusades of Valencia's Conquest (1225–1280): An Historiographical Labyrinth," in *Social Origins of Medieval Institutions*, 167–77, esp. 167–72.

38

When Men of Vassals May Be Considered Vassals of the Sovereign and When They May Not Be, and In What Things They are Bound to the Sovereign and In What to Their Lord

Barons, such as counts, viscounts, vasvassours,[51] and the like, as well as other simple knights, who are vassals of the sovereigns of the land, may have certain vassals under their authority, because of the fiefs which they hold for the sovereign of this land. Such vassals are themselves the sovereign's men, both by the right of fealty and by the general jurisdiction that the sovereign exercises over his own realm. The baronial vassals can never direct their own men against the sovereign himself, but he, as lord, can use their own vassals against the barons. These baronial vassals possess other vassals because of their own freeholds, and these are not tied to the sovereign by homage, since they are not under his authority. Thus, while these vassals are not under obligation to the sovereign because of fealty and homage, yet they are said to be under his authority because of the general jurisdiction which he holds in his kingdom. Indeed, he holds authority over all the subjects of his kingdom.[52]

Thus everything in his realm is the king's in regard to his jurisdiction over it. Thus, if any baron in the sovereign's land rises in rebellion against him, and the baron orders his vassals to help him against the sovereign because of the oaths of fealty which he had received from him, they are not bound to help the baron since he is seriously delinquent in duty and has committed the crime of lèse-majesté.[53] Thus, when the baron himself is seriously delinquent, his vassals, even

---

[51] The vasvassour was "a vassal of a vassal" defined by the legists Joan Blanch and Jaume Callis as "a baron or captain who held fiefs and vassals under such nobles." *Usatges*, trans. Kagay, 65; Socarrats, *Commemorationes*, 408.

[52] For concepts of levels of jurisdiction in medieval law and political theory, see J. P. Canning, "Introduction: Politics, Institutions and Ideas," *Cambridge History of Medieval Political Thought*, 350; Berman, *Law and Revolution*, 114–15, 205–15, 255–69, 308–10.

[53] Although this Roman concept of treason made its way into the codes of Norman Sicily and England, it was replaced by the term *traison* in France, where, according to Philippe de Beaumanoir, it meant the harboring of a "deadly hatred" which impelled one to seek a secret, dishonorable vengeance. In Catalonia, treason, with few exceptions, was rendered by the term *bausia*, which implied a "default of service," such as a vassal's failure to answer a lord's military summon, his desertion of his lord on the battlefield, his assault

those whom he has from his own freeholds, are not bound to help him, and even his direct order does not excuse them from their duty to the sovereign. The vassals whom the baron has from fiefs he possesses from the sovereign are even less obliged to help him. For in more dangerous matters, neither they nor their vassals have to obey their lord. The bond imposed by the oath of fealty does not tie them in such matters, since no obligation can be established for shameful ends. This is true when any baron rises in rebellion against his lord without any preceding legal claim or litigation. But if the sovereign unjustly causes damage to a baron who is his vassal by removing fiefs or freeholds without entering a legal claim, then the baron, after filing suit with his lord, can summon the vassals of his freeholds to help him against the sovereign if, by rising in rebellion, he wishes to defend himself. Thus, in accordance with the custom of Catalonia, the vassals of his freeholds are bound to help their lordly vassal.[54]

---

on the lord or a member of his family, or some sexual misconduct with the lord's wife or daughter. The usual lordly response to *bausia* was the immediate confiscation of the *bauzator*'s castle or fief. Crook, *Law and Life of Rome*, 252–53; Janet Nelson, "Kingship and Empire," *Cambridge History of Medieval Political Thought*, 223; Berman, *Law and Revolution*, 420–21; *Coutomes de Beauvaisis*, 303, no. 826; *The Establissements de Saint Louis: Thirteenth-Century Law Texts From Tours, Orléans and Paris*, trans. F. R. P. Akehurst (Philadelphia, 1996), 105–6, no. 171; John Hudson, *The Formation of the English Common Law: Law and Society from the Norman Conquest to Magna Carta* (London, 1996), 161; *Usatges*, trans. Kagay, 70–72, 74, arts. 25, 30–31, 39; Kagay, "Structures," 66.

[54] To demonstrate the crown's normal and predictably vehement response to such a course of private justice, Socarrats cited an order of the vicar of Gerona which forbade landholders from serving as a militia or judicial agents. Socarrats, *Commemorationes*, 408.

39

In Which Ways Vassals Whom Barons Hold Under their Authority, as well as Freeholders, and Other Subjects Are Tied to the Sovereign

If any baron of the king of Aragon (for instance, the count of Empúries)[55] wages war against any of his neighbors who is not a native of the lord king's land (for instance Amaury of Narbonne)[56] or the king of Aragon/count of Barcelona wages war on the king of Castile or the Saracens (who have attempted to occupy the kingdom of Valencia or remove any other of his lands from him), and then the count of Empúries orders his vassals to aid him against Amaury of Narbonne; and finally the king also commands his vassals to aid him against the king of Castile, who was attempting to subjugate his land, or against the Saracens, who were trying to do the same thing: in this case (though some of the vassals were from the count's freeholds and some from the fief that the count holds from his lord, the king of Aragon), all of these men, who are normally subject to the count from freehold or fief, are obliged to obey the king of Aragon and not the count. Indeed, the vassals, who are summoned for the sake of public utility, have an excuse in following the greater over the lesser authority, since public utility must be preferred to private.[57] In this case, then, the vassals are bound to obey the king and

---

[55] This Pyrenean noble house, which centered on the old Roman town of Ampurias, was linked with the viscounties of Bas and Bearne by marriage in the thirteenth century. When all these branches died out in the late thirteenth century, a second dynasty of Empúries began with a cadet line of the Barcelona house. Sobrèques, *Barons*, 90–91, 132–38.

[56] In all likelihood, this refers to Arnaud Amaury, abbot of Citeaux, general of the Cistercian Order, archbishop of Narbonne, and papal legate to southern France during the first stages of the Albigensian crusade. He led a contingent of French knights across the Pyrenees and took part in the crushing, Christian defeat of Spanish Islam at Las Navas de Tolosa in 1213. Defying both the counts of Toulouse and the Papal crusaders, Simon and Amaury de Montfort, Amaury retained his ecclesiastical post and political power until his death in 1225. Joseph R. Strayer, *The Albigensian Crusades* (Ann Arbor, MI, 1994), 57–58, 62–64, 90–91, 101–2, 126–27, 144.

[57] This maxim had a long history in Roman law, originating in Stoic thought and receiving a logical treatment in the legal works of Cicero. The importance of the "common good" (*publica utilitas*) and its predominance over private advantage was used in a number of medieval juridical settings, including the investiture struggle between the pope and the Holy Roman Emperor and between the same German emperors and the Italian towns. By the mid-thirteenth century, the statement had become a truism among a reading public,

not the count. Since the king summoned these vassals so his realm would not be conquered, or so he would not lose some of its territory, and therefore he summoned them for the good of, and in the name of, the country over which he holds sway, they must obey such a royal order and, because of this obligation, fight for their country.[58] In this case, it is permissible for these vassals to oppose

---

even that portion of which was not formally trained in Roman law. See Henry Procopé, "Greek and Roman Political Theory," in *Cambridge History of Medieval Political Thought*, 21–36, esp. 24; D. E. Luscome and G. R. Evans, "The Twelfth-Century Renaissance," in *Cambridge History of Medieval Political Thought*, 306–38, esp. 311; Anthony Black, "The Individual and Society," in *Cambridge History of Medieval Political Thought*, 588–606, esp. 596; Pennington, *Prince and the Law*, 71, 233–35; Catherine Moriarity, *The Voice of the Middle Ages in Personal Letters 1100–1500* (New York, 1983), 53.

[58] Although the basis of general military service to the count of Barcelona was laid out in article 64 of the *Usatges*, which begins with the words *Princeps namque*, it seemed to raise more questions than it answered. In regard to persons bound to the count by feudal ties, was their service unlimited, and did they have to serve wherever the sovereign led them? Or, like residents of a castle, was their military participation territory-sensitive and not required outside Catalonia? Although homage and the grant of a fief enforced on the vassal a "contract of service" as Jaume de Marquilles observed, such service was neither universal nor unlimited. Men with small fiefs were exempt from military duty, and even those, like the viscount of Cardona, who had a clear duty to serve could refuse to go to war, unless they were paid a salary and had all their losses on campaign reimbursed. In regard to freeholders, *Princeps namque* clearly mandated their participation in defense of the realm. But did this mean that peasants would be armed? The dangerous implications of such an action, though occasionally indulged in during such desperate times as the period of French invasion of 1284–1285, was recognized by Catalan monarchs from Pere III onward. Their fears of an armed peasantry became all too real during the *remença* wars of the fifteenth century.

In jurisprudential terms, one of the most significant questions connected with *Princeps namque* centered on who could invoke the power. Following the letter of the *Usatges*, legists and vassals alike questioned the general military summonses that were not issued by the sovereign himself. With the increasing absence of the Catalan ruler from Catalonia owing to official business in the other realms of the Crown of Aragon, the appointment of lieutenants from the royal family or officialdom to rule Catalonia became usual, but their right to issue a general military summons, even during periods of true emergency, was questioned by legists, parliaments, and the Catalan vassals themselves. The answer to this quandary definitely varied with point of view. From Jaume I onward, the Catalan rulers argued that their legitimate sons could administer Catalonia in their name. The sovereign also felt that they could call out armies for him, especially if there truly was a national emergency. The royal position was perhaps best expressed by Pere III who, during the bitter conflict with Jaume III of Majorca, claimed that "it was never tolerated by the princes of Catalonia

or even kill their own fathers, if they rose up against the king.[59]

Therefore in such situations when one is fighting for his country, these vassals can defy the orders of their lord, the count, especially since the king issued this order for the sake of public utility and public utility must be preferred to private. Yet even though the count of Empúries may hold these vassals by a twofold right of obligation (namely, the right of jurisdiction which he holds over them and that of homage), yet, despite this twofold right, they are not under obligation to the count, since a valid point can far outweigh two less valid ones. Nevertheless, it cannot be denied that the these vassals must obey the count of Empúries if the king summons them for a matter which does not affect public utility. The objection should not be raised in this case that the vassals are summoned by a greater authority.[60] Even though in individual terms the king is greater than the count, he is notwithstanding not greater in respect to these vassals, and as far as they are concerned, the count is greater, since the king maintains only one right of obligation over them: namely, that of the general jurisdiction which he exercises over them and not the right of homage as discussed above.

---

that foreign warriors should be in the Principate to make war and the barons and knights should harbor such a pestiferous act [of refusing the general summons]." The nobles and townsmen, who would bear the cost of such enforced military aid, sought to limit such expeditions to those commanded by the ruler; they consistently refused to honor campaigns summoned by members of the royal family or administrative agents. The ultimate exception of this type was discussed by legists of the fifteenth century, who wondered if persons had to answer such a general summons, if the king intended to wage an unjust war with the assembled troops. Socarrats, *Commemorationes*, 358–400, 420; Tomás Mieres, *Apparatus super Constitutionibus curiarum generalium Cataloniae* (Barcelona, 1621), fol. 163v; Alvarrolis, *Super Feudis* (Venice, 1477), 472.

[59] For the literary and legal changes in the status of fatherhood from Carolingian times onward, see Riché, *World of Charlemagne*, 60–61; David Herlihy, *Medieval Households* (Cambridge, MA, 1985), 127–30; Beatrice Gottlieb, *The Family in the Western World from the Black Death to the Industrial Age* (New York, 1993), 236, 257.

[60] For distinction of "pure" and "mixed authority" (*merum, mixtum imperium*) as defined in the Middle Ages, see Kenneth Pennington, "Law, Legislative Authority and Theories of Government, 1150–1300," in *Cambridge History of Medieval Political Thought*, 424–53, esp. 432; idem, *Prince and the Law*, 20–21, 213–14; *Notule*, 159, doc. 425, Burns, *Islam*, 268–70.

THE CUSTOMS OF CATALONIA

40

That an Overlord Cannot Buy a Fief or Inferior Castellany Attached to His Castle

If in any castle a lord had two castellans, one of whom was of a higher rank than the other, the first [higher-ranking] castellan would hold the castle for the overlord and render homage to him, while the second would remain there, rendering homage to the first castellan for the castellany or fief. If in this situation the inferior castellan wishes to sell to the overlord the castellany which he held from the first castellan, the overlord, according to the law, usage, and custom of Catalonia, cannot buy the inferior castellany, but has to follow the order prescribed by the law, usage, and custom of Catalonia. Thus, the first castellan is bound to render homage to the overlord for this thing and fief, and this same lord would be feudatory or vassal of his own vassal or feudatory in regard to this castle or fief. Thus, if the vassal should render homage to the overlord who was of a higher rank than he, and if the greater lord should render homage to his vassal because of the castle or fief sale, then the vassal would be considered superior his lord and this is not allowed. For this reason, a lord cannot buy such a fief or inferior castellany. If the second vassal wants to sell a fief which he holds from the first vassal to a lord of a higher rank by some privilege, he can do this if the first vassal, the one who granted the inferior fief, gave his consent and it was sold as a freehold. Thus the lord king, Pere [I], father of the current king Jaume, granted the *leudas*[61] of the Seu [cathedral] of Barcelona as a fief to Lord Guillem de Mediona,[62] who sold them as a freehold to Lord Berenguer, bishop of Barcelona, as

---

[61] The *leuda* was an impost charged by the king or local baronial or clerical authority on goods brought to a local market for sale. The Catalan tax was similar to a Castilian tax known as the *portazgo*. Valdeavellano, *Instituciones españoles*, 607; Miguel Angel Ladero Quesada, *Fiscalidad y poder real en Castilla (1252–1369)* (Madrid, 1993), 131–39.

[62] Guillem de Mediona, a retainer of Pere I, emerged as one of the wealthiest Barcelona citizens by selling the vicarate of the city back to the crown in 1205. In the next decade, he extended his power through the purchase of an important strip of the capital's coastline and through marriage which brought the control of several significant castles, most important of which was Castellet in the Penedés district. He remained an important courtier in Jaume I's early years, serving in the young king's earliest military campaigns and in a number of parliaments. The peak of royal approval occurred in January, 1222 when de Mediona received the lucrative contract for the collection of the *leuda* for Barcelona and its environs. This was granted in a document referred to as "memorandum of *leudas* sealed

the overlord of the *leudas*. This sale was made as a freehold to the overlord, and the lord king Pere, from whom Guillem de Mediona held them, confirmed it with an official document.

in public form and divided by the letters of the alphabet." *DJ*, 1:77–85, doc. 34; Bensch, *Barcelona and its Rulers*, 218–19; *Fiscal Accounts*, ed. Bisson, 1:256; 2:doc. 167, pp. 300–1; Miret i Sans, *Itinerari*, 31, 40, 56, 96, 117, 151.

41

Whether the Nephew of a Vassal Who Died Without a Male Heir Can Become the Vassal of the Lord of the Fief After Acceding to the Feudal Holding, and Concerning the Time Period During Which the Nephew or Some Heir of the Deceased Vassal Must Come Before the Lord of the Fief [to Claim it]

If any vassal who does not have a son but does have a nephew, dies intestate, and the nephew who is the successor of this intestate vassal accedes to the deceased vassal's feudal holding, and is made a vassal of his dead uncle's lord, then the nephew must renew homage and render fealty to the lord. Indeed, just as one who accedes to an inheritance is under obligation to all of the deceased's creditors, so a person who accedes to a feudal holding is similarly obliged to the lord by right of homage. The nephew thus takes on the legal identity[63] of the deceased, and should come before the lord of the fief and say: "Lord, I am the heir of so-and-so, your dead vassal, and the fief which he once held for you has passed down to me. I wish to render homage and renew fealty to you." Certainly, if the lord accepts him as vassal and bestows the fief on him, and it afterwards happens that someone else comes and claims that he was clearly more closely related to the deceased vassal, saying that he should succeed to the fief, the acceptance as vassal that the lord extended to the first party should not prejudice the case of the person

---

[63] "Legal identity" (*persona*) was a tradition which stretched back to early medieval times and into Justinian's laws, attributing to the sovereign the role of "natural lord" of the realm. As law became more sophisticated with the spread of Roman codes during the twelfth century, the distinction between the ruler and the office he exercised became better defined. With the thirteenth century, the legalism of rule had reached such currency that Jaume I could describe himself and his sons as "one conjoint person," whose bodies made up "the body of the kingdom." This concept of the king's "twofold" nature was quickly adapted to many other political explanations. Thus, the "people" of cities and states were routinely differentiated from the individual. This same type of doctrine was quickly apparent in the corporation, which stood as "legal fiction" (*ficta persona*), acting as one person, but composed of many. In this and the following article of Pere Albert's work, a similar distinction is made between the person and office of a son and his father and between a fief and the vassal who holds it. *LF*, 2:138, chap. 141; Maravall, *Pensamiento*, 1:133; Kantorowicz, *King's Two Bodies*, 87–97; Strayer, *Medieval Origins*, 53–54; Pennington, "Law," 474–76.

who came later for it seems clear that the lord had received the first party with the rank of vassal, had granted him the right to the fief, or had invested him with it, on condition it was due him or had to belong to him. But if a nephew or the closest relative of a vassal who passed away with or without a will does not come before the lord of the fief to renew homage and fealty within the proper time limit — that is, within a year and a day — but comes after this time limit has elapsed, the lord must decide whether this relative loses or keeps the fief. Likewise, the lord can sue against this heir forcing him to recognize that he had held the fief from him for more than a year and a day.

This is the general custom of Catalonia: whoever is the heir of a deceased vassal, whether he died with or without a will, must come before the lord of the fief within a year and a day, prepared to renew or render homage and fealty to the lord of the fief. Unless he does so, he must lose the fief, if the lord is favor of this. But if the heir claimed that he abandoned the fief to the lord because, by this renunciation or desertion of the fief, he wanted to avoid rendering homage to the lord of the fief, he, according to Roman law and reasonable custom, cannot evade his responsibility to the fief by such a desertion since he assumed the legal identity of the deceased vassal, from whom he acceded to the feudal holding and retained it for such a long period. Just as the deceased vassal could not during his lifetime evade the responsibility of homage by abandoning the fief without the consent of the lord, so his heir — whoever he may be — who wishes to abandon the fief cannot free himself from homage, but must render it to the lord of the fief after he, the heir, has received to the deceased vassal's feudal holding from the lord of the fief and held it for the stated period. Indeed, the heir must renew fealty, for because he promised fealty to the lord for the fief and assumed the legal identity of the deceased, he rendered homage for the legal identity of deceased vassal to the lord of the fief. Even though the same words are said as above, yet this is not a new promise of fealty, but rather a certain type of renewal of a long-standing homage.

42

How a Crime Committed Against a Lord by a Vassal May or May not Prejudice the Son of the Vassal So That the Son May Not Succeed to the Fief

A crime committed against the lord of a fief by a vassal may or may not legally prejudice this vassal's son. Indeed, if the father who committed the crime had commended himself as a vassal for the fief which commenced with him (that is, if such a feudal holding was newly given to this vassal or he bought it), in this case, the fief begins with him and his crime would legally prejudice his son's position, since the son could not succeed to this fief except through the legal identity of his father. So, like the father who, as a vassal, committed a crime against his lord and was therefore expelled from his fief, so his son will be expelled from the fief. But if the fief does not commence with the father, but instead had begun to be a fief from the time of the grandfather, the vassal's father, and if this grandfather was still living and the son of the guilty vassal had not yet been born, in this case the vassal's crime will not legally prejudice his son's position, since no punishment for this case can apply from the grandfather's legal identity, since no line of consanguinity had been established between the son and the grandfather. Yet, if the grandfather was living and the son of the guilty vassal had been born, and afterwards (while the grandfather was still living) the father and vassal committed a crime against the lord of the fief, then the crime that he committed will not legally prejudice his son's position, since he [the son] does not want to be invested with this fief from the legal identity of his father who had committed the crime, but instead from the legal identity of his grandfather. Therefore, in this case, it was as if the father and guilty vassal did not exist in a line of succession between the son and the grandfather. But if it was after the grandfather had died that the vassal had committed the crime against his lord, in this case the crime is prejudicial to the son of the guilty vassal, since from the time of the grandfather's death the father, who served as vassal for the fief, was next of kin and able to succeed. Thus, with his son excluded, the vassal would succeed to the fief, since he was the next of kin. This is also true if the vassal, the son's father, had acceded to the feudal holding of his own father, the son's grandfather. Otherwise, if the father, after committing the crime, did not repudiate the feudal holding or did not accede to it, then the son, despite the crime his father had committed, can succeed his grandfather and hold the fief through the legal identity of his grandfather. Yet the son cannot succeed to the fief through the legal identity of his father, for in this case the son would have been automatically rendered delinquent and expelled from the fief.

43

Which and How May Are the Rights
That a Lord Has Over His Vassals

If any liege lord has a liege vassal, he may claim certain things from him because of the jurisdiction of homage; thus this vassal is subject to the jurisdiction of his liege lord, and the same person stands as his judge. Thus all the property of the liege vassal which he does not hold from another lord as a non-liege fief is subject to the liege lord because of his jurisdiction. Even though the liege vassal does not hold such property from his lord as a fief, it is clear that, after he has totally subordinated his person to his liege lord, all his property is also subject to the lord. Nevertheless, it must not be thought that, because of this, the lord possesses the same mixed or pure authority over his liege vassal that the sovereign of the land has, even though, as just stated, the lord has jurisdiction over the vassal and his possessions.

But, if one is not a liege lord of a vassal nor a liege vassal of a lord, then the lord has no greater jurisdiction over his non-liege vassal than that afforded him from the fief that this vassal holds for the lord. Therefore this is the difference between a liege and a non-liege vassal: a liege vassal totally binds himself in his legal identity to his lord, even though some property referred to as a fief may involve the renunciation of such rights. Thus, by totally subordinating his legal identity to his lord because of the liege fief, he then subjects all his property to his lord. I do not claim that the lord can receive such a subordination from the basis of the liege fief, even though he can claim it from the jurisdiction he holds. Yet a non-liege vassal does not bind his legal identity. Thus he is subordinated to the jurisdiction of his non-liege lord only as much as the terms of the fief bind him to this lord. Consequently, he may exercise as much power in general terms as this specific case allows him. Likewise, the vassal cannot publicly accuse his lord of a crime, nor summon him before the law without his permission, nor can a vassal accuse his lord, unless he is seeking redress for a grievance against himself or his own vassals.[64] Likewise, he must help his lord against his enemies, and he certainly must

---

[64] The question of vassalian litigation against a lord was limited not only by the lord's consent, but also by the venue chosen to have such differences aired. Some legists, such as Jaume Callis, claimed that a litigation site could be chosen anywhere in the lord's land and, once this site was specified on the judicial summons, it could not be challenged. Other authorities, such as Jaume de Montjuich, declared that the litigation had to take place in the county or bishopric in which the vassal lived, or if it was moved from this district,

help him against all men, except for certain exceptions (that is, a father against his son, grandson against grandfather and vice versa), for the lord cannot order his vassal to aid him against such persons because such action is contrary to good customs.

Likewise a vassal must put the life of his lord over his own; for if the lord has to fight a duel,[65] say, if someone wishes to prove by judicial combat against him that he committed the crime of *lèse-majesté* or some other offense, the lord can surely order his vassal or one of his vassal's men to undergo this combat in his place. Likewise, a vassal must give sustenance to his lord when in need and, unless he does so, the vassal may be viewed in this case as wishing to harm his lord.

Likewise a vassal cannot sell his fief without the consent of his lord. Yet if the lord gives his consent but does not himself want to buy back the fief, the vassal can sell it to another of equal or greater rank than he. Thus if the vassal and seller is a knight, he must sell the fief to a knight of equal rank and not to a townsman

---

there could be a change of venue only to a district in which the vassal owned property or held a fief. Socarrats, *Commemorationes*, 448–49, 460–63.

[65] Springing from the "wager by battle" (*batallia*), the "duel" (*duellum*) had a long history in Catalonia and in other Iberian realms that stretched well into the early modern period. Although the form was outlawed by the Church in the Fourth Lateran Council of 1215 and by such Catalan rulers as Pere III who claimed that the duel was against "divine . . . canon and civil law," duels took place at all levels of eastern Spanish society. The most important duel of early Catalonia's history was at the heart of Pere II's attempt to end hostilities with France in 1285 by challenging to single combat the French prince, Charles of Anjou. Even though challenges to duels were originally delivered personally or in writing by the last centuries of Iberian dueling, such calls to the vindication of personal honor could be secretly posted, thus allowing the aggrieved party to attack his enemy at his leisure and often from ambush. Such illegal private warfare also thrived among the nobles and townsmen of Catalonia to such an extent that the form was molded by customary feudal and Roman corporate influences. Thus it was not unusual for vassals to be called on to serve as substitutes for their lords on the dueling field, or for town councils to act as middlemen in arranging for and carrying out individual duels. Although the duel was slowly eradicated in Spain between the Catholic Kings and the Bourbons, it remained sufficiently strong, even when condemned by royal lawyers, to give rise to a code of dueling customs, the *code duello*. Socarrats, *Commemorationes*, 471–83; Henry Charles Lea, *The Duel and the Oath*, ed. Edward Peters (Philadelphia, 1979), 105–6; Bernat Desclot, *Chronicle of the Reign of King Pedro III of Aragon*, trans. F. L. Critchlow (Princeton, 1928), 103–18, chaps. 31–31; Francesch Carreras i Candi and Siegfried Bosch, "Desafiaments a Catalunya en el Segle XVI," *BRABLB* 16 (1933–1936): 39–64, esp. 46–47; Fernando Valls Taberner, "Notes sobre el duel judicial a Catalunya," idem, *Obras*, 2:247–57; Kagay, "Iberian *Diffidamentum*," 73–82.

or even to a knight of lower rank. But if he does so, the lord is not bound to accept as vassal a townsman or a knight of lower rank, and can confiscate the fief if the vassal is guilty of such an act. If he does not want to do so, he can opt to retain the seller as his vassal; for through such a substitution (that is, the sale of his fief to a townsman or to someone of rank inferior to his), the seller is not considered freed from the responsibility of the homage to his lord. It is considered just in Catalan custom and Roman law for a seller to substitute one of equal or greater, but not of lesser rank, than himself.

Likewise, according to the letter of the law, a feudatory cannot sell or alienate his fief, whether his lord consents to this or not, since in homage one cannot substitute a buyer. Thus it is fitting that the seller of the fief should be substituted for, but that the buyer should render homage to the lord, since feudal property is always transferred with the responsibilities attached to it; namely, in rendering homage, renewing fealty, and posting bonds whenever requested by his lord, in aiding him against his enemies, and in carrying out all other duties that a feudatory must perform for his lord. Likewise, if the seller is a liege vassal of the lord for whom this fief is held, and who consents to its sale, it is fitting that the buyer should be made the liege lord, from whom the fief is held. In addition, the vassal cannot sell the fief to this buyer unless the lord consents. Therefore according to custom — and here it harmonizes with equity — even though a lord disapproves of the sale of the fief, as mentioned above, the vassal himself can still sell it to a man of equal or greater rank.

Likewise, if any vassal or feudatory does not want to render that service to his lord which is due him, the lord, on his own authority, can demand before his court the service of homage, just as a father is within his rights to chastise his son. Yet if the lord is not certain whether the feudatory from whom he seeks service is his vassal, the person from whom this service is sought should comport himself like a freeman, and not as if he were the lord's vassal. In this case, the lord cannot render judgement against him, but the dispute must be referred to an ordinary judge. Likewise, whenever there was a dispute between lord and vassal or feudatory, the terms of the agreement that were established with the granting of the fief must be adhered to and observed, and such disputes must be settled in accordance with the feudal pact.

Likewise whenever any baron or lord gives a fief to another and says the following words to him: "I grant to you, _ and to your heirs, _ such and such a fief," no one in this case must succeed this feudatory except those directly related to him. The lord, in granting the fief, must be seen as recognizing only those descendants of the person to whom the fief was granted and not others who were not direct descendants.

Likewise, if any man who never had a wife dies without a will, his lord must not exact a third of his property or anything else because of his intestacy. This is decreed in the article of the *Usatges* which refers to intestates.[66] Likewise, if after the intestate death of a peasant, a vassal, a knight, or any other villager whose son did not have a settled abode in any village or royal castle but lingered for short periods in one place or another, the lord of this man's father, and not the king or even the village in which his father died, must have a third of the deceased's property. This is decreed in the above-mentioned article of the *Usatges*.

---

[66] *Usatges*, trans. Kagay, 94, art. 117.

44

When and How a Lord May Confiscate Control of Another's Castle for Default of Service or When He May Not

The custom of Catalonia is as follows: if, because of vassalian default of service or failure to post bond, any lord takes over castle control or confiscates a fief that was held for him, the vassal should come before his lord and say the following words: "Lord, I am now prepared to post bond." Even though the vassal may have refused his lord on several occasions or wished to have the case concerning his default of owed service or the refusal to post bond for his lord submitted to the investigation of a judge appointed by his lord, yet, the lord, on the other hand, does not have to accept either this bond or restore control of the castle if he held it, or give back the fief which he had confiscated, or even return to his vassal any revenues he may have collected in these sites, until this vassal reimburses him twice over for any additional damage and expenses he may have incurred. Like-wise, the vassal should guarantee his lord that he will not from then onward refuse to render the service he owes or post bond for him. Once this is done, the lord must return control of the castle or fief — if he has confiscated them — to his vassal. Nevertheless, the lord is not bound to return to his vassal the revenues he collected there.

45

Concerning the Refusal of a Vassal or Castellan to Post Bond For a Lord From Whom he Directly Held the Castle, and How the Other Fiefholders Must Respond

Likewise, the custom of Catalonia is as follows: if there are two, three, or more vassals of a castellan or feudatory in any castle, and the overlord makes any demand from the castellan who immediately holds the castle from him, and the castellan does not want to assume legal responsibility for his lord by posting bond nor then to render fealty and homage and, because of this, the overlord confiscates from him the castle and the fief, then the other castellans who held a fief from the first castellan (the person who refused to assume legal responsibility for the overlord by posting bond or by rendering fealty) must themselves post bond with their lord and issue against the first castellan a list of grievances: namely, that he should have assumed legal responsibilities for the overlord or entered into litigation, rendered homage or performed any other duties that he is reasonably required to do for the overlord. They should do this to avoid losing their fiefs because of their own lord's guilt, even though they were not in agreement with him and considered it a serious offense to refuse the demands of one's overlord. If the castellan, who is lord to the others, persists for a year, a month, and a day in his refusal to render homage or to carry out any duty that his own lord reasonably demands, the castellan who holds the fief directly from the first lord and castellan (the person who does not want to render homage or carry out those things which are reasonably required to maintain one's fief) should come before the overlord and render homage and accept the fief from him under the same conditions that the first castellan had. In this case, the overlord cannot refuse to accept his homage or return the fief to him, even if the castle lord is deprived of a vassal. It was decreed in the *Book of Fiefs* that if a feudatory failed for a year, a month, and a day to render homage to his lord for a castle or a fief which he holds for him, he will lose the fief forever,[67] even though he was not warned or his lord did not enter a legal claim concerning the fief, since the vassal must present himself and personally render homage. Nevertheless, the custom of Catalonia decrees that he should not lose the fief, unless it was legally claimed by the lord and, after this claim was filed, the vassal still refused to render homage for a year, a month, and a day. After this period, the vassal will then lose his fief.

---

[67] *Libri Feudorum*, 519–20, II, tit. X, xiii–xxiv.

46

How a Fief Held by Two, Three, or More
Should be Divided Among Them

Care must be taken if, by chance, there are two, three, or more lords holding a fief for another.[68] If the lowest in rank or any other of middling rank should wish to sell the rights or jurisdiction that he has there, the pledges, bonds, thirds, and fief-transfer fees should wholly and completely accrue to the overlord, and thus the others, even as castellans and feudatories, cannot collect any of these revenues. Nevertheless, according to the custom of Catalonia, as soon as a fief is sold or transferred, the lord for whom it is held must have a guaranty there and collect a third or a fief-transfer fee from the seller. Likewise, he must divide these receipts into three portions, retaining two-thirds of them for himself, while giving the other third to the other lords. Thus, from a third of fief-transfer fee of nine *sous*,[69] he will retain six *sous* and give the others three. These three *sous* should be divided in this way: two *sous* should be given to the lord for whom the fief was directly held and twelve *dinars* to the overlord from whom the fief was held. The division must be made in this way from one lord to the other, but if there happen to be more lords, two-thirds should accrue to the man with the closest tie to the overlord. It is also the custom of Catalonia that if a fief is sold, the lord from whom the fief is immediately held can retain for himself as much as the lord who

---

[68] Socarrats declared that a fief or castellany was essentially alienable and divisible. Its benefits and revenues could be claimed by all who received a portion of the tenure. The *laudemium* or fee for subinfeudating all or part of a fief normally accrued to the overlord, but could be claimed by the castellans who might be strapped for cash. Because all revenues for such holdings were supposed to accrue to the overland, division of these rents could be construed as a violation of the feudal pact which bound the overlord to his principal vassal. To avoid this problem, the first vassal would make supposedly-independent grants to his own vassals from the body of feudal revenues he controlled. This situation was further complicated when clerical institutions acted as overlords. They often bestowed fiefs on vassals in exchange for annual cash payments. When these men tried to recoup their losses for such fief payments, a steady proliferation of subvassals or under-castellans resulted. When the clerical institutions as overlord stepped in, a complicated and expensive round of litigation followed — all to determine how much of the revenue base went to the overlord and how much could be claimed by the lesser tenants. Socarrats, *Commemorationes*, 548–58.

[69] See introduction note 171.

is selling the fief wishes to give him, despite the objections of the overlord or the other lords about this. And this is so since the fief is diminished by one knight, and thus, in this case, such objections do not apply to this lord because the fief of the lord who held it as a guaranty was lost. Therefore, from the nature of this fief, the lord from whom the fief was immediately held must post bond and retain the third. Nevertheless, the lord who retains this fief for himself should retain none of the revenues.

47

How Any Castellan Can Refuse to Render Homage
If the Lord Sells the Fief to Someone
of a Lower Rank Than the Castellan

The custom of Catalonia is as follows: if a lord sells his castle to a person of lower rank than he, but if the seller and buyer are both knights, the castellan who held the castle for the seller may try to avoid rendering homage to the buyer of the castle instead of the seller, so as not to be forced to have a lord of a lower rank. Yet in this case he is bound to render an oath of fealty, and because of this oath of fealty which he already took to the seller, he is bound to post bond, surrender castle control, and perform all services, as if had rendered homage to the buyer. The same applies in regard to a townsman, villager, or anyone else who buys a castle. Nevertheless, if the knight who buys the castle is a noble, whom the castellan can serve without insult, dishonor, blame, or treason, then he is bound to render homage for the fief, even though the seller was of a higher rank than this buyer.

48

Whether a Vassal Can Remove a Fief From a Lord

The custom of Catalonia is as follows: a vassal cannot remove a fief from a lord; similarly, a lord cannot remove a fief from a vassal without reasonable cause. However, if a vassal or feudatory designates a successor, to whom he bequeaths his fief, the successor can repudiate and abandon the fief to the lord. If, however, the successor has either rendered homage, posted bond, surrendered castle control, rendered service, or made use of the fief in some way after the death of the first lord, he cannot abandon this fief, since in these cases he has subsequently made use of it.

49

Whether a Lord Can Claim a Fief-Transfer Fee From the Successor to a Fief Who Granted To His Brother or Sister a Portion of His Inheritance, or of a Lawfully-Held Castle, Village, Revenue, or Tithes

The custom of Catalonia is as follows: if a father having two, three, or even more sons should make a will designating one as heir and bequeathing or designating a certain sum of money to the others, and the heir does not want to or does not have the money to pay them, he may grant from his portion or inheritance to his legitimate brother or sister a castle, estate, tithe, or rent attached to his fief. If the brother or sister agrees to a monetary settlement with him, in this case the lord for whom the fief was held can claim a third, a fief-transfer fee, or other things customary with a sale. This action is, indeed, a sale, even though the charter refers to it as a grant. In such a fief, the lord from whom the fief is directly held can make legal claims on the vassal for up to thirty years. Nevertheless, there are certain cases in which he cannot do so. In the matter of the property which the heir grants to his brother or sister, the lord may receive a bond or service after the grant was conferred on them just as if the lord himself had conferred this grant on the brother or sister. If there was an overlord, intermediate castellans, or feudatories there, such a claim does not apply to them, but only to the vassal directly tied to the overlord. Nevertheless, if a third or fief-transfer fee was collected from the brother or sister for this holding, the lord with the closest tie to the overlord from whom the fief is directly held must receive two-thirds of the revenues and the other third should be divided among the other lords.

50

Whether a Vassal Can Divide His Fief

The Roman law and custom of Catalonia are as follows: no one can divide a fief among his children or other persons without his lord's consent. Nevertheless, if a vassal takes possession of two or three fiefs for a lord concurrently or at different times, he can validly bequeath them to or divide them among different persons. Yet no one on his own can break up a fief, manor, castle, revenue, or any other thing held as a fief.

51

Whether or Not Residents or Freeholders of Free Status Are Bound to Render Labor Service Within the Boundaries of Any Castle as Other Vassals Are

The custom of Catalonia is as follows: if two or three estate tenants who are freeholders of free status live within the boundaries of any castle, or in its surroundings, and the lord of the castle has a war, or anticipates having one, these tenants — even though their land be not bound to any knight or church — are required to work on the walls, on the picket lines, on the outer walls, on the barbicans, and on the archer points. They are also bound to aid in setting ambushes, in manning the walls, in serving as guards and in garrisons, in mustering out to every battle signal of the castle, and even in participating in combat within all the castle boundaries. If, in such an engagement, any person of the castle or his property should be captured, the tenant must help free him or get back his property. But if anyone is wounded or killed in such combat, the tenant is not bound to him as a vassal. Moreover, if one goes out beyond the boundaries of the castle and is captured, the tenant does not have to rescue him, nor retrieve his property, but the resident can act to ransom him and his property. The freeholder cannot be excused from doing any of these things, even though he may claim that his estate is outside the castle boundaries, and it can be defended without the help of the castle.

52

When a Castellan Should be Bound to Render an Oath of Homage to the Overlord, and When a Sub-Castellan is Bound to Do the Same

The custom of Catalonia is as follows: if there is a sub-castellan in any castle, and even though the castellan has rendered homage and fealty to the overlord, this same overlord can then demand that the sub-castellan also render homage and fealty to him. This is so even if such a sub-castellan happens to be a freeholder and estate tenant with his own fortified house within the castle boundaries: the overlord can demand homage and fealty from him to prevent such a person from causing damage to the lord, or to any of the men of the castle because of control of the entry or exit, or of his estate.

53

Whether a Knight Must Render Homage to Another Knight for His Fief, That is, For Fiefs Worth Twenty Sous or Less

The custom of Catalonia is as follows: for a fief worth twenty *sous* or less, a knight does not have to render homage unless it was then customary to do so or if it had been agreed upon between the parties in the following way: the lord should take the vassal by the hand, and he should promise to be a faithful and law-abiding vassal for the fief, and post bond as was customary with fiefs of this value. Yet for such a small fief he does not have to render homage.

54

Whether a Vassal Has to Render Homage When There Are Two Heirs in One Castle, and Each Demands That His Vassal Render Homage to Him For His Portion

The custom of Catalonia is as follows: if a freeholder and lord of a castle has two sons, and divides this castle into two portions, designating one portion for one son and the second portion for the other, and if each son for his portion of the castle demands homage, castle control, the posting of a bond, or anything else that must be done for a fief, his vassal is not bound to carry out these things unless he renders homage to one of the brothers, and they agree which of them would receive this homage and for whom the vassal is obliged to engage in litigation, post bond, surrender castle control, render service, and do all the other things customarily done for a fief. But if the heirs do not come to such agreement, the homage is still valid, and the vassal does not have to disavow any of the actions that he had taken.

55

Whenever There Are Many Freeholders In One Castle, How Many Must Render Homage to the Others

The custom of Catalonia is as follows: if there are two or three freeholders in the same castle, homage must be rendered between them in the following way: one should clearly establish himself under the authority of the other and subordinate himself to him, while he is within the boundaries of the castle or village. But in the time of peace and war, one of these freeholders is not bound to serve in the castle garrison with the others; and if one of them does not wish to do this, the others can force him to do his duty in accordance with the oaths made by the lord of the land.[70]

---

[70] Catalan custom asserted that this kind of group responsibility could extend even to the formal division of fines or penalties caused by the crimes of one of the members of the group. Romanist legists, strongly influencing royal statutes, claimed that it was legally untenable for members of a group who were completely innocent of a crime to share punishment for it simply because of an earlier agreement with the malefactor. Socarrats, *Commemorationes*, 296.

56

These Are the Cases According to the Usatges of Barcelona and Observances of Catalonia In Which a Lord is not Bound to Return the Control of a Castle or Fief That He Has Confiscated from a Castellan

The first case is when a vassal has refused to post bond and the lord, because of this or any other default, seizes control of the castle by force: then the lord is not bound to return control of a castle or any fief, if he has confiscated these from the vassal for this reason, until the vassal posts bond and renders homage in the above-mentioned form to the lord and reimburses him for all the costs that he incurred while seizing the castle.

The second case is when a lord has had a war with his vassal or with anyone else: since it was then necessary to maintain possession of the castle because of the war, the lord is not obliged to restore castle control that he had taken over as long as the war lasts.

The third case is when a castellan refuses to surrender castle control to his lord as he is obliged to, and the lord seizes by force the castle as well as all the fiefs subject to it that the castellan held: then the lord is not bound to return the castle or those fiefs until the castellan reimburses his lord for all the expenses and damages that the lord incurred with the seizure and garrisoning of the castle, and until the castellan has assured his lord that he will refrain from hostile action by swearing an oath and asserting in a public document that from then on control of this castle will not be refused to him.

The fourth case is when a castellan or vassal refuses to render to his lord service which he was bound to do to the best of his ability or in accordance with custom, and, because of this refusal, the lord confiscates this fief or receives castle control: then the lord is not bound to return the fief or castle until the vassal has rendered the aforesaid service to him twice over and gave full assurance by bond that he will not from then on refuse service.

The fifth case is when a vassal going to war along with his lord deserts him on the battlefield while still alive and runs away or otherwise dishonorably fails his lord in combat: then because of this the vassal loses his castle and all fiefs that he held for the lord. In this case, the lord is not bound to return these holdings to him.

The sixth case is when a vassal haughtily breaks off feudal ties or abandons his fief to his lord: then the lord can confiscate everything the vassal had held from him until he shall render homage, post bond, and make amends to him by oath for the dishonor he has done him.

The seventh case is when a lord has to hold a castle for some certain part of the year in accordance with the feudal agreement made between himself and the castellan to whom castle control was given: and ten days after the lord has taken control of the castle (after which time, according to the custom of Catalonia, control had to be returned to the castellan), the castle control may be extended to the time limit prescribed in the feudal agreement. During or after this time, the period of ten days will commence. The lord can hold the castle for this ten-day period, but once it has passed he must return the castle, unless any situation from the preceding cases should emerge that would prohibit the lord from returning the castle control.

The eighth case is when a vassal has refused to obey his lord, and with great contumacy, contempt, and effrontery has broken feudal ties with his lord: then the vassal must forever lose all fiefs and benefices that he holds and controls for the lord without any hope of ever recovering these, unless the lord freely restores these to him. If the vassal should also have possessed some chattels and immovable property not connected to the fief, and if he was requested by the lord before he committed the crime of refusing to render service to his lord, he must render the service that he had delayed or refused, even if he has lost his own property with the fief.

There is likewise another case, the ninth, in which the lord king can retain control, that is, when the lord king and his vicar sue any of the magnates, knights, or any other person for the restoration of peace and truce and wish them to post bond for the payment of the *bovatge*,[71] he may also wish to retain control of the castle until the malefactor has made amends for all the wrong, damage, and distraint which committed against the lord because of this, in accordance with that contained in the constitution of the peace and truce, which begins "If any of the magnates."[72]

---

[71] *Bovatge*: a tax imposed on the owners of cattle, which from the time of Pedro II was associated with the maintenance of stable coinage. Bisson, *Conservation of Coinage*, 88–91, 98–100; Ferran Soldevila, "A proposit del servei del bovatge," *AEM* 1 (1954): 753–87.

[72] *Usatges*, trans. Kagay, 70–71, art. 25

Appendix: Consuetudo Barchinonae

This short guidebook to the adjudicative customs of Barcelona has long been attributed to Pere Albert, though the following version was included in such later works as the thirteenth-century edition of the great Catalan privilege of 1284, the *Recognoverunt proceres*, and a fourteenth-century collection of cases and legal customs of Catalan law by Guillem Vallseca, legal adviser to several Aragonese monarchs.[1] The principal manuscripts in which this short legal handbook are included generally comprise collections of Catalan law, including the *Usatges* or *Commemoracions*. The most important of these manuscripts are:

Paris, Bibliothèque National, MS. Lat. 4672.
Real Biblioteca de San Lorenzo de Escorial, MS. Z, I, 4.
Arxiu de la Corona d'Aragó, Monacales, Santa María de Ripoll, MS. 23.

The only modern edition is that by Ferran Valls-Taberner, "Un articulat inèdit de Consuetuds de Barcelona," idem, *Obras*, 2:140–47.

The Customs of Barcelona

1. The Custom of Barcelona is that the court retains a third of the expenses of a litigant, who was judged guilty, but it must not retain a third of the bonds. In a judgement, the question of expenses should be agreed upon with the party declared guilty and his court costs should be reimbursed to him. The custom is observed differently in other places.
2. It is the custom that the overlord should fully retain for himself a fourth of all sales, even though it was elsewhere observed that he should retain a third. Thus when the seller keeps 200 *sous*, I, as overlord, get 100. It is

---

[1] *Gran Enciclopedia Catalana*, 18 vols. (Barcelona, 1969–1993), 15:266–67; *Diccionari Biogràfic*, 4 vols. (Barcelona, 1969), 4:420.

observed differently elsewhere, since from the 300 *sous*, the lord would retain a third, that is 100 *sous,* not in full right, but as an emphyteusis. He would also keep another 50 *sous* as a bond.

3. The custom is also such that a person can appeal an interlocutory sentence on the same day.

4. The custom is also such that a person may appeal a judgement on the same day.

5. Likewise, even though bonds are posted or promised under penalty in a judgement, nevertheless one cannot with impunity appeal to a higher court unless this was expressly declared and recognized as an appeal, or if the case was called up to the higher court and was accompanied with the penalty money or bonds of the lower court. This is the custom of Barcelona.

6. A litigant may not be forced to pay court costs, if he cannot obtain them [from his adversary].

7. A person may be considered a tenant of an *exorchia*[2] from the age he can father children.

8. The Custom of Barcelona and other places is such that a lord should have a third of the property of the tenant of an *exorchia*, as is stated in the articles of the *Usatges* "Concerning the holders of *exorchias* and intestates" and "I otherwise sanction."[3]

9. After a knight's son is twenty years old, he should no longer receive revenues from such lands. Before his twentieth birthday, he should receive these every four years. Indeed, a peasant's son should not receive these revenues after his fourteenth birthday.

10. Likewise, if my estate controls the tenure of another's estate, a peasant cannot sell this tenure without my consent unless it was patently obvious that he held it for another lord. Indeed, then the consent of that lord is sufficient, regardless of the fact that this tenure is controlled by my estate. Then my peasant, and not I, as lord of the estate, will have the third [for the sale].

11. Likewise, if my peasant has a freehold which was always within the tenure

---

[2] An *exorchia* was feudal or allodial land of a person who died childless. A third of the land of such a tenant who happened to be a noble or townsman reverted to the sovereign; that of a peasant was claimed by his immediate lord. An *intestia* was the land of a tenant who died without a will, which was claimed, in part, by his overlord. *Usatges*, trans. Kagay, 80, 86, arts. 65, 86; Rodón Binué, *Lenguaje técnico de feudalismo*, 108–9.

[3] See preceding note.

of my estate, he cannot sell it without my consent; then he must give me a third of the sale price if it was still in his possession. Likewise, I declare that if it is clear that the land sold as a freehold truly is one, I will never have a third even after a hundred years. Thus I decree this is true since it must be observed that one cannot sell a certain property, no matter at what time it was acquired unless it was beyond human memory, i.e., in cases like that of "Concerning rainwater," Article 1.1 [*Liber Judiciorum*] at the end.[4]

12. Likewise, concerning the legal obligation of a bond, the lord should have a tenth in place of a fief-transfer fee, and this is in accordance with the custom of Barcelona. Thus for the price of one *onza*,[5] 12 *dinars* should be given to the lord.

13. The custom of Barcelona is that a peasant can leave the land after satisfying his obligations to his lord.

14. Likewise, if a husband has settled a nuptial grant on his wife, even though the wife did not grant her husband her dowry, the heir of this marriage must return the nuptial grant to the wife after the husband's death. This is in accordance with the custom of Barcelona, even though it is contrary to Roman law.[6]

15. The custom of Barcelona is such that during the period of a contract dating from when the value of money was greater than at the present time and though it states that it should be settled at current monetary levels, nevertheless it should be settled as the king ruled twice or three times over to the money's current value. But if the contract was made in terms of the money that was then circulating, then it may be claimed that the sum should be paid in accordance with the money's current level of circulation and should not be repaid twice over.

16. The custom of Barcelona is such that except in the cases of a fief that one holds for the king, or those of homicide, the royal ban, the capture of a robber, theft, battery which causes bloodshed, and in other similar cases, the accused must be heard before an ordinary judge though one is not prohibited from going to another judge. With associations, partnerships and in similar arrangements, any judge can preside.

---

[4] *LV*, 344–45, VIII, 4, 30–31.

[5] A gold coin of Muslim Valencia which began to circulate in Catalonia in the late eleventh century. *Usatges*, trans. Kagay, 69, 76.

[6] Compare with *Justinian's Institutes*, trans. Bieks and McLeod, 83, 2, 20, 15.

17.   The custom of Barcelona is such that a royal vicar,[7] who is transferred, and his substitute, must equally share between themselves the bonds and sureties held for judicial reasons. The first vicar will retain half of these, but the substitute vicar will keep none of these, except when ordered to by the first vicar. The substitute vicar will, however, collect all judicial bonds and sureties.

18.   The custom is also that, even though the lords should make an out-of-court settlement, nevertheless, if the royal vicar settles a dispute between peasants, he will make a ruling in this case, no matter what the lords had agreed on.

19.   The custom is also such that a vassal must not abandon his fief, but a peasant can leave the land, according to the custom of Barcelona; but in certain other places they customarily cannot leave the land.

20.   Likewise, certain authorities say that a lord cannot seek a fief-transfer fee at the same time that he exacts or deducts a tenth from an inheritance.

21.   Likewise, if a husband assigned a castle as a wedding gift to his wife, even if it is in lieu of a monetary payment, I declare that the wife, for up to a year after her husband's death, may claim these properties and any other that may appear.

22.   Likewise, if a feudatory or even a peasant gives to his wife the wedding gift of a fief or land that he holds for his lord without the lord's knowledge or express consent, the lord, after the death of the feudatory or peasant, can legally seize this land and expel the wife. But when a vassal or peasant gives a dowry for his daughter or a wedding grant for his son, that which he held for his lord remains in effect, even if the lord was unaware or did not consent to this.

23.   Likewise, after it has been confirmed under the authority of the king, his vicar, his bailiff. or anyone else of the court that, if litigants agree among themselves without the permission of the court, each party will grant to the court as much as the plaintiff could claim from a defendant. When this sum has been handed over, then the settlement will be ratified. But if they cannot pay, each will be given one hundred lashes, and the judge may termi-

---

[7] The royal vicar (*vicarius, veguer*) was a Catalan official whose history dated back into the twelfth century. The vicar emerged from being a protector of the sovereign's peace to one of the foremost territorial administrators who often oversaw the collection of taxes, the administration of justice, and the deployment of troops. Lalinde Abadia, *Jurisdicción real inferior en Cataluña,* 52–55, 173–83.

nate this case for the second time. And all of this is declared in the Gothic laws, bk. II, tit. II: "If after anyone is held captive."[8] But when a crime is involved, such a sentence is not valid, and 5 *sous* should be presented for contempt, as this case is dealt with in the seventh book under "If anyone for a crime."[9] But one may avoid this penalty if he made a settlement with the permission of the court and in accordance with the fiftieth book "If one is taken captive."[10]

24. A feudatory can give a fief to his son without the knowledge or consent of his lord, since, when he acquired the fief for himself or his son, he nevertheless caused no prejudice to his lord.

25. Likewise, even though a father should settle a dowry on his daughter and afterwards left nothing to her in his will, or did not make a will, she should inherit as the Roman laws[11] declare, since there is no custom contrary to this even though there are certain authorities who have opposite opinions.

26. The custom of Barcelona is such that if a vassal has a castle within the county of Barcelona and the lord lives in another county or wishes his vassal to come into another county to answer legal charges there, the lord cannot do this: and this was so judged in the case between B. de Podio vs B. de Gardiola. The same was judged in the case between the lord king and G. de Cardona[12] in which the king wished G. to come into Aragon, so he might engage in litigation with him there. It was ruled that he could not and must not go out of the county even under an oath by which he ceased hostilities.

27. Or it was thus declared: "I thus concede to you and your progeny, posterity and offspring that they have succeeded and descended from an intestate." And this is approved from custom.

---

[8] *LV*, 79, II, 1, 32.

[9] *LV*, 66, II, 1, 19.

[10] *LV*, 287, VII, 1, 4.

[11] *Justinian's Institutes*, trans. Birks and McLeod, 65, 2, 7, 3.

[12] Guillem de Cardona (1177–c.1226), adviser of Pere I "the Catholic, who survived the disastrous defeat at Muret to become one of Jaume I's most important early advisers. Despite their importance as courtiers, Cardona and his successors became some of Jaume's most fractious nobles who engaged in intermittent skirmishes and almost constant litigation with the Crown. Sobrequès, *Barons*, 100–2; John Shideler, *A Medieval Catalan Noble Family: The Montcadas (1000–1230)* (Berkeley, 1983), 144–45; Kagay, "Structures of Baronial Dissent," 62–63.

Bibliography

Primary Sources

Antiquiores Barchinonensium Leges, quas vulgus Usaticos appellat commentariis supremorum jurisconsultorum Jacobi a Monte judaico, Jacobi & Guilermi a Vallesicca et Jacobi Calici. Barcelona, 1544.

Beaumanoir, Philippe de. *The Coutumes de Beauvaisis,* trans. F. R. P. Akehurst. Philadelphia, 1992.

Bracton, Henry de. *On the Laws and Customs of England,* trans. Samuel E. Thorne. 4 vols. Cambridge, MA, 1977.

Caffaro, *De captione Almerie et Tortuose,* ed. Antonio Ubieto Arteta. Valencia, 1973.

Canellas López, Angel. "Fuentes de Zurita. '*Anales,* III: 66–67': Las asambleas de Calatayud, Huesca y Ejea en 1265." *Cuadernos del historiador Jeronimo Zurita* 31–32 (1992): 12–41.

Capitularia Regum Francorum. Monumenta Germaniae Historica. Legum: sectio II, ed. Alfred Boretius and Victor Krause. 2 vols. Hanover, 1907.

Cartas de población y franquicia de Cataluña, ed. José María Font Rius. 2 vols. Madrid–Barcelona, 1969.

Cartulario de Sant Cugat de Vallès, ed. José Rius Serra. 3 vols. Barcelona, 1945–1947.

Colección de las cortes de los antiguos reinos de Aragón y de Valencia y el principado de Cataluña, ed. Fidel Fita y Colomé and Bienvenido Oliver y Esteller. 27 vols. Madrid, 1896–1922.

Colección de documentos inéditos del Archivo General de la Corona de Aragón, ed. Prospero de Bofarull y Moscaró. 42 vols. Barcelona, 1850–1856.

Compilación del derecho civil especial de Cataluña. Ley de 21 de Julio 1960. Barcelona, 1962; repr. Barcelona, 1984.

Constitutiones y altres drets de Cathalunya compilats en virtut de capitol de cort LXXXII de las corts del Rey Don Philip IV nostre senyor celebradas en la ciutat de Barcelona any MDCCII. Barcelona, 1704; repr. Barcelona, 1973.

Constitucions de Catalunya, ed. José María Font Rius. Barcelona, 1988.

Crónica de San Juan de la Peña, ed. Antonio Ubieto Arteta. Valencia, 1961. trans. Lynn H. Nelson, *The Chronicle of San Juan de la Peña. A Fourteenth-Century Official History of the Crown of Aragon*. Philadelphia, 1991.

Cubells, Manuel. "Documentos diplomáticos aragoneses (1259–1284)." *Revue Hispanique* 27 (1916): 105–250.

The Digest of Justinian, trans. Alan Watson, 2 vols. Philadelphia, 1998.

Diplomatarium of the Crusader Kingdom of Valencia: The Registered Charters of the Conqueror Jaume I, 1237–1276. ed. Robert I. Burns, S.J. 2 vols. to date. Princeton, 1991– .

Documenta Selecta Mutuas Civitatis Arago-Cathalaunicae et Ecclesiae Relationes Illustrantia, ed. Johannes Vincke. Barcelona, 1936.

Documentos de Jaime I de Aragón, ed. Ambrosio Huici Miranda and María Desamparados Cabanes Pecourt. 4 vols. Valencia, 1976–1978.

The Establissements de Saint Louis: Thirteenth-Century Law Texts From Tours, Orléans and Paris, trans. F. R. P. Akehurst. Philadelphia, 1996.

El fuero latino de Teruel, ed. Jaime Caruana Gómez de Barreda. Teruel, 1974.

Feudal Society in Medieval France: Documents from the County of Champagne, trans. Theodore Evergates. Philadelphia, 1993.

Fiscal Accounts of Catalonia under the Early Count-Kings (1151–1213), ed. Thomas N. Bisson. 2 vols. Berkeley, 1984.

Fori Antiqui Valentiae, ed. Manuel Dualde Serrano. Madrid, 1950–1967.

El fuero latino de Teruel, ed. Jaime Caruana Gómez de Barreda. Teruel, 1974.

Los fueros de Aragón, ed. Gunnar Tilander. London, 1937.

Galbert of Bruges. *The Murder of Charles the Good*, trans. James Bruce Ross. Toronto, 1959; repr. Toronto, 1988.

Gesta comitum barchinonensium. Textos llatí i català, ed. Louis Barrau-Dihigo and Jaume Massó Torrents. Barcelona, 1925.

The History of Feudalism, ed. David Herlihy. New York, 1970; repr. New York, 1971.

Justinian's Institutes, trans. Peter Birks and Grant McLeod. Ithaca, NY, 1987.

Leges Visigothorum. Monumenta Germaniae Historica. Legum: sectio I, ed. Karl Zeumer. Hanover, 1902.

Liber Feudorum Maior, ed. Francisco Miguel Rosell. 2 vols. Barcelona, 1945–1947.

Libri Feudorum [Feudorum Consuetudines Partium ex Editione Vulgata in Codicis Justiniani D. N. Sacratissimi Principis pp. Augusti Repetitae Praelectionis Libri XII]. Lyons, 1662.

Llibre dels fets del rei En Jaume, ed. Jordi Bruguera. 2 vols. Barcelona, 1991.

El "Llibre Blanch" de Santes Creus, ed. Federico Udina Martorell. Barcelona, 1947.

Marca hispanica sive limes hispanicus, hoc est, geographica et historica Cataloniae, Ruscinonis, et circumiacentium populorum, compiled by Pierre de Marca, ed. Etienne Baluze. Paris, 1688; repr. Barcelona, 1972.

Mieres, Tomás. *Apparatus super Constitutionibus curiarum generalium Cataloniae.* Barcelona, 1621.

Pere III of Catalonia, *Chronicle (Crònica)*, trans. M. Hillgarth, ed. J. N. Hillgarth. 2 vols. Toronto, 1980.

The Register "Notule Communium 14" of the Diocese of Barcelona (1345–1348), ed. J. N. Hillgarth and Giulio Silano. Toronto, 1983.

Socarrats, Johannes de. *Tractatum Petri Alberti canonici barchinonensis de consuetudines Cataloniae inter dominos et vassalos ac nonnullis aliis que commemorationes Petri Alberti appellantur.* Barcelona, 1551.

Traducción al Castellano de los Usajes y demas derechos de Cataluña, ed. and trans. Pedro Nolasco Vives y Cebria. 4 vols. Madrid, 1861; repr. Barcelona, 1984.

Los Usatges de Barcelona y els Commemoracions de Pere Albert, ed. Josep Rovira i Ermengol. Barcelona, 1933.

The Usatges of Barcelona. The Fundamental Law of Catalonia, trans. Donald J. Kagay. Philadelphia, 1994.

Vidal, Pedro, *Anales de la Orden de Predicadores, 1172–1228,* Biblioteca Universitaria de Barcelona, MS. 748–49.

The Voice of the Middle Ages in Personal Letters 1100–1500, ed. and trans. Catherine Moriarity. New York, 1983.

Secondary Sources

Abadal i de Vinyals, Ramón d'. "Les partidas y Catalunya." *EUC* 6 (1912): 13–37, 161–81.

———. *Pere el Ceremoniós i els inicis de la decadència política de Catalunya*. Barcelona, 1972.

Amelang, James S. *Honored Citizens of Barcelona: Patrician Culture and Class Relations*. Princeton, 1986.

Aragó, Antonio M., and José Trenchs Odena. "Las escribanías reales catalano-aragonesas de Ramón Berenguer IV a la minoría de Jaime I." *RABM* 80 (1977): 421–42.

Arco y Garay, Ricardo del. "El jurisperito Vidal de Canellas, obispo de Huesca (noticias y documentos inéditos)." *Cuadernos de Historia Jeronimo Zurita* 1 (1951): 23–113.

————. "Nuevas noticias biográficas del famoso jurisperito del siglo xiii, Vidal de Cañellas, obispo de Huesca." *BRABLB* 9 (1917): 221–49; 10 (1921): 83–113.

Aunós Pérez, Antonio. *El derecho catalán en el siglo XIII.* Barcelona, 1926.

Bachrach, Bernard S., and David Nicholas, eds. *Law, Custom, and the Social Fabric in Medieval Europe: Essays in Honor of Bryce Lyon.* Kalamazoo, MI, 1990.

Bagnall, Roger. "Slavery and Society in Late Roman Egypt." In *Law, Politics, and Slavery in the Ancient Mediterranean World,* ed. B. Halpern and D. Hobson, 220–40. Sheffield, 1993.

Balari Jovany, José. *Orígenes históricos de Cataluña.* 2 vols. Barcelona, 1909; repr. Abadía de San Cugat del Vallés, 1964.

Barbero, Abilio, and Marcelo Vigil. *La formación del feudalismo en la peninsula ibérica.* Madrid, 1978; repr. Barcelona, 1986.

————. *Sobre los orígenes sociales de la Reconquist.* Barcelona, 1979; repr. Barcelona, 1988.

Barrero, Ana Maria. "El derecho romano en los 'Furs' de Valencia de Jaime I." *AHDE* 41 (1971): 639–64.

Bartlett, Robert. *The Making of Europe: Conquest, Colonization and Cultural Change 950–1350.* Princeton, 1993.

Bensch, Stephen P. *Barcelona and its Rulers, 1076–1291.* Cambridge, 1995.

Benson, Robert L., and Giles Constable, eds. *Renaissance and Renewal in the Twelfth Century.* Cambridge, MA, 1982.

Berman, Harold J. *Law and Revolution: The Formation of the Western Legal Tradition.* Cambridge, MA, 1983.

Bishko, Charles Julian. "The Spanish and Portuguese Reconquest." In *A History of the Crusades,* ed. Kenneth M. Setton et al. 4 vols. 3:396–457. Madison, WI, 1962–1975.

Bisson, Thomas N. "The Crisis of Catalan Franchises (1150–1200)." In *Formació,* 153–72.

————. *Conservation of Coinage: Monetary Exploitation in France, Catalonia and Aragon, c.1000–1225 A.D.* Oxford, 1979.

————. "Feudalism in Twelfth-Century Catalonia." In *Structures féodales et féodalisme dans l'Occident méditerranéen, X^e–XIIIe siècles: bilán et perspectives de recherches,* 172–92. Rome, 1983.

————. *The Medieval Crown of Aragon: A Short History.* Oxford, 1986.

————. "The Organized Peace in Southern France and Catalonia, ca. 1140–ca. 1230." *AHR* 82 (1977): 290–303.

————. "The Problem of Feudal Monarchy: Aragon, Catalonia, and France." *Speculum* 53 (1978): 466–78.

————. "Ramon de Caldes (c.1135–c.1200): Dean of Barcelona and King's Minister." In *Law, Church, and Society: Essays in Honor of Stephan Kuttner*, ed. Kenneth Pennington and Robert Somerville, 281–92. Philadelphia, 1977.

————. *Tormented Voices: Power, Crisis, and Humanity in Rural Catalonia, 1140–1200*. Cambridge, MA, 1998.

Black, Anthony. "The Individual and Society." In *Cambridge History of Medieval Political Thought*, 588–606.

Bloch, Marc. "European Feudalism." In *Theories of Society: Foundations of Modern Sociological Theory*, ed. Talcott Parsons et al. 2 vols. 2:385–92. New York, 1961; repr. New York, 1965.

————. *Feudal Society*, trans. L. A. Manyon. 2 vols. Chicago, 1966.

Blythe, James M. *Ideal Government and the Mixed Constitution in the Middle Ages*. Princeton, 1992.

Bois, Guy. *The Transformation of the Year One Thousand*. Manchester, 1992.

Bonnassie, Pierre. *La Catalogne du milieu du XIe à la fin du XIe siècle: croissance et mutation d'une société*. 2 vols. Toulouse, 1975–1976. trans. Jean Birrell, *From Slavery to Feudalism in South-Western Europe*. Cambridge, 1991.

————. "Un contrat agraire inédit du monastère du Sant Cugat (28 août 1040)." *AEM* 3 (1966): 444–50.

————. "Les conventions féodales dans la Catalogne du XIe siècle." In *Les structures sociales de l'Aquitaine, du Languedoc, et de l'Espagne au premier âge féodal*, 187–208. Paris, 1969.

————. "Du Rhone a la Galice. Genèse et modalités du regime féodal." In *Structures féodales*, 17–55.

————. "A Family of the Barcelona Countryside and its Economic Activities Around the Year 1000." In *Early Medieval Society*, ed. Sylvia Thrupp, 103–27. New York, 1967.

————. "Sur la formation du féodalisme catalan et sa première expansion (jusqu'à 1150 environ)." In *Formació i expansió del feudalisme català*, 7–21. Gerona, 1985–1986.

Breen, Quirinius. "The Twelfth-Century Revival of Roman Law." *Oregon Law Review* 24 (1944–1945): 244–85.

Broca y Montagut, Guillem Maria de. *Historia del derecho de Cataluña*. Barcelona, 1918; repr. Barcelona, 1985.

————. "Juristes i jurisconsuls catalans del segles XI, XII, y XIII. Fonts del seus coneixements y transcendència." *Anuari de l'Institut d'Estudis Catalans* 2 (1908): 429–42.

Brown, Elizabeth A. R. "The Tyranny of a Construct: Feudalism and the Historians of Medieval Europe." *AHR* 79 (1974): 1063–89.

Brundage, James A. *Medieval Canon Law*. London, 1995.

Brynteson, William E. "Roman Law and Legislation in the Middle Ages." *Speculum* 41 (1966): 420–37.

Burns, Robert I., S.J. "Canon Law and the Reconquista: Convergence and Symbiosis in the Kingdom of Valencia under Jaume the Conqueror (1213–76)." In *Proceedings of the Fifth International Congress of Medieval Canon Law*, 387–424. Vatican City, 1980.

———. *The Crusader Kingdom of Valencia: Reconstruction on a Thirteenth-Century Frontier*. 2 vols. Princeton, 1967.

———. *Islam under the Crusaders: Colonial Survival in the Thirteenth-Century Kingdom of Valencia*. Princeton, 1975.

———. "The Many Crusades of Valencia's Conquest (1225–1280): An Historiographical Labyrinth." In *Social Origins of Medieval Institutions*, 167–77.

———. "The Spiritual Life of James the Conqueror: Portrait and Self-Portrait." In X *CHCA*, Comunicaciones, 1–2:323–58.

———, ed. *Emperor of Culture: Alfonso X the Learned of Castile and his Thirteenth-Century Renaissance*. Philadelphia, 1990.

———, ed. *The Worlds of Alfonso the Learned and James the Conqueror: Intellect and Force in the Middle Ages*. Princeton, 1985.

———, and Paul E. Chevedden. "'The Finest Castle in the World'." *History Today* 49, no. 11 (November 1999): 10–17.

———, and Paul E. Chevedden. *Negotiating Cultures: Bilingual Surrender Treaties in Muslim Christian Spain*. Leiden, 1999.

Burns, J. H., ed. *The Cambridge History of Medieval Political Thought, c.350–c.1450*. Cambridge, 1988.

Butt, Ronald. *A History of Parliament: The Middle Ages*. London, 1989.

Camps Arboix, J. *La masia catalana*. Barcelona, 1959; repr. Barcelona, 1976.

Canellas López, Angel. "Fuentes de Zurita. '*Anales*, III: 66–67': Las asembleas de Calatayud, Huesca y Ejea en 1265." *Cuadernos del historiador Jeronimo Zurita* 31–32 (1981–1982): 12–41.

Canning, Joseph. *A History of Medieval Political Thought, 300–1450*. London, 1996.

Carreras i Candi, Francesch. *Geografia general de Cataluña, La ciutat de Barcelona*. Barcelona, 1916.

———. "La institució del castlá en Cataluña." *BRABLB* 1 (1901–1902): 4–23.

———. *Miscelánea histórica catalana*. 2 vols. Barcelona, 1905–1918.

——— and Siegfried Bosch. "Desafiaments de Catalunya en segle XVI." *BRABLB* 16 (1933–1936): 39–64.

Castro, Américo. *The Spaniards: An Introduction to Their History*, trans. Willard F. King and Selma Margaretten. Berkeley, 1971.

Chevedden, Paul E. "The Artillery of King James I the Conqueror." In *Iberia and the Mediterranean World in the Middle Ages*, ed. Paul Chevedden, Donald Kagay, and Paul Padilla, 47–94. Leiden, 1996.

Cheyette, Fredric L. "The Invention of the State." In *Essays on Medieval Civilization*, ed. Bede K. Lackner and Kenneth R. Philp, 143–78. Austin, 1978.

Clanchy, Michael T. *From Memory to Written Record, 1066–1307*. Oxford, 1979; repr. Oxford, 1993.

Claramunt, Salvador. "Els Estudis Generals i la transmissió de saber." In *Pere el Cerimoniós i la seva època*, ed. Maria Teresa Ferrer i Mallol, 151–60. Barcelona, 1989.

Coing, Helmut, ed. *Handbuch der Quellen und Literatur der neuren europäischen Privatrechtsgeschichte*. Vol 1: *Mittelalter. Die Gelheten Rechte und die Gesetzgebung*. 3 vols. in 7 parts. Munich, 1973–1988.

Collins, Roger. *The Arab Conquest of Spain, 710–797*. London, 1989.

Comellas, José Luis. *Historia de España Moderna y Contemporanea (1474–1975)*. Madrid, 1985.

I Congrés d'història de la corona d'Aragó, dedicat al rey en Jaume I y la seva època. 2 vols. numbered as one. Barcelona, 1909–1913.

VII Congrés d'història de la corona d'Aragó. 3 vols. Barcelona, 1963–1964.

X Congrés d'història de la corona d'Aragó. Jaime I y su època. 3 vols. Zaragoza, 1980.

Contamine, Philippe de. *War in the Middle Ages*, trans. Michael Jones. New York, 1987; repr. Oxford, 1990.

Crook, J. A. *Law and Life of Rome 90 B.C.–A.D. 212*. Ithaca, NY, 1967.

Daly, L. J. *The Medieval University*. New York, 1961.

Danús, Micaela. "Conquesta y repoblación de Mallorca: Notas sobre Nicoláu Bovet." In X *CHCA*, Comunicaciones, 1–2:41–64.

Debord, Andrè. "The Castellan Revolution and the Peace of God in Aquitaine." In *The Peace of God: Social Violence and Religious Response in France around the Year 1000*, ed. Thomas Head and Richard Landes, 135–64. Ithaca, NY, 1992.

Diccionari biogràfic. 4 vols. Barcelona, 1966–1970.

Donahue, Charles. "Law, Civil." In *Dictionary of the Middle Ages*, ed. Joseph R. Strayer et al. 13 vols., 7:418–25. New York, 1982–1989.

Dualde, Manuel, and José Camarena. *El compromiso de Caspe*. Zaragoza, 1980.

Duggan, Charles. "Papal Judges Delegate and the Making of the 'New Law' in the Twelfth Century." In *Cultures of Power: Lordship Status and Procession in Twelfth-Century Europe*, ed. Thomas N. Bisson, 172–202. Philadelphia, 1995.

Elías de Tejada, Francisco. *Las doctrinas políticas en la Cataluña medieval.* Barcelona, 1950.

––––––. *El pensamiento político de los juristas catalanes medievales.* Madrid, 1948.

Engels, Odilo. *Schutzgedanke und Landesherrschaft im östlichen Pyrenäenraum (9.–13. Jahrhundert).* Munich, 1970.

Erickson, Carolly. *The Medieval Vision: Essays in History and Perception.* New York, 1976.

Evergates, Theodore. *Feudal Society in the Bailliage of Troyes under the Counts of Champagne, 1152–1284.* Baltimore, 1975.

––––––. "Nobles and Knights in Twelfth-Century France." In *Cultures of Power,* 11–35.

Ferrer i Mallol, Maria Teresa. *La Frontera amb Islam en el Segle XIV: Cristians i Sarrains al Pais Valencià.* Barcelona, 1988.

––––––. "La frontera meridional valenciana durant la guerra amb Castella dita del Dos Pere." In *Pere el Cerimoniós i la seva època,* 260–75. Barcelona, 1989.

Font Rius, José María. "La comarca de Tortosa a raiz de la reconquista cristiana (1148)." *CHE* 19 (1953): 104–28.

––––––. "El desarrollo general del derecho en los territorios de la Corona de Aragón." In VII *CHCA,* 1:289–326.

––––––. "The Institutions of the Crown of Aragon in the First Half of the Fifteenth Century." In *Spain in the Fifteenth Century,* 172–92.

––––––. "Origenes del regimen municipal de Cataluña." *AHDE* 16 (1945): 389–529; 17 (1946): 229–589.

Freed, John B. "Constitutio de Feudis." In *DMA,* 3:557–58.

Freedman, Paul. "Catalan Lawyers and the Origins of Serfdom." *Mediaeval Studies* 4 (1986): 288–314

––––––. "The Enserfment Process in Medieval Catalonia: Evidence from Ecclesiastical Sources." *Viator* 13 (1982): 225–44.

––––––. *The Origins of Peasant Servitude in Medieval Catalonia.* Cambridge, 1991.

García y García, Antonio. "La penetración del derecho clásico medieval en España." *AHDE* 36 (1966): 575–93.

García Sanz, Arcadio. "El 'Corpus juris civilis' en els documents dels segles xii–xiv." *Ausa* 6 (1969): 89–102.

Glick, Thomas F. *From Muslim Fortress to Christian Castle: Social and Cultural Change in Medieval Spain.* Manchester, 1995.

González Antón, Luis. *Las cortes de Aragón.* Zaragoza, 1978.

––––––. *Las uniones aragonesas y las Cortes del reino (1283–1301).* 2 vols. Zaragoza, 1975.

Gottlieb, Beatrice, *The Family in the Western World from the Black Death to the Industrial Age*. New York, 1993.

Gouron, André. "Aux origines de l'influence des glossateurs en Espagne." In *Études sur la diffusion des doctrines juridiques médiévales*. Study VI, 325–46. London, 1987.

———. "Gênes et le droit provençal." In idem, *Études*, 7–15.

———. "La science juridique française aux XIe et XIIe siècles: Diffusion du droit de Justinien et influences canoniques jusqu'à Gratien." In idem, *Études*, Study 2, 3–118.

Gran Enciclopedia Catalana, 18 vols. Barcelona, 1969–1993.

Guterman, Simeon. *From Personal to Territorial Law: Aspects of the History and Structure of the Western Legal Constitutional Tradition*. Metuchen, NJ, 1972.

Haskins, Charles Homer. *The Renaissance of the Twelfth Century*. Cambridge, MA, 1939; repr. New York, 1972.

Helmholtz, R. H. *The Spirit of Classical Canon Law*. Athens, GA, 1996.

Hennessy, C. A. M. *The Federal Republic in Spain: Pi y Margall and the Federal Republican Movement, 1868–74*. Oxford, 1962; repr. Westport, CT, 1980.

Herlihy, David. *Medieval Households*. Cambridge, MA, 1985.

Highfield, Roger, ed. *Spain in the Fifteenth Century 1396–1516*, trans. Frances M. López-Morillas. New York, 1972.

Hinojosa y Naveros, Eduardo de. "La admisión del derecho romano en Cataluña." In idem, *Obras completas*. 3 vols. 2:389–401. Madrid, 1948–1974.

Hudson, John. *The Formation of the English Common Law: Law and Society in England from the Norman Conquest to Magna Carta*. London, 1996.

Humphries, Paul Douglas. "Of Arms and Men: Siege and Battle Tactics in the Catalan Grand Chronicles." *Military Affairs* 49 (1985): 173–78.

Kagan, Richard L. *Lawsuits and Litigants in Castile (1500–1700)*. Chapel Hill, NC, 1981.

Kagay, Donald J. "Army Mobilization, Royal Administration and the Realms in the Thirteenth-Century Crown of Aragon." In *Iberia and the Mediterranean World*, 95–116.

———. "The Emergence of 'Parliament' in the Thirteenth-Century Crown of Aragon: A View from the Gallery." In *On the Social Origins of Medieval Institutions: Essays in Honor of Joseph F. O'Callaghan*, ed. Donald J. Kagay and Theresa M. Vann, 223–41. Leiden, 1998.

———. "The Iberian *Diffidamentum*: From Vassalic Defiance to the *Code Duello*." In *The Final Argument: The Imprint of Violence on Society in Medieval and Early*

Modern Europe, ed. Donald J. Kagay and L. J. Andrew Villalon, 73–82. Woodbridge, Suffolk, 1998.

———. "The King's Right Must be Preferred to the Lord's: Sovereignty and Suzerainty in the Treaties of Pere Albert." *Proceedings of the Tenth International Congress of Medieval Canon Law*. Forthcoming.

———. "*Princeps namque*: Defense of the Crown and the Birth of the Catalan State." *Mediterranean Studies* 8 (1999): 1–32.

———. "Royal Power in an Urban Setting: James I and the Towns of Crown of Aragon." *Mediaevistik* 8 (1995): 127–36.

———. "Structures of Baronial Dissent and Revolt under James I (1213–76)." *Mediaevistik* 1 (1988): 61–85.

———. "Two Towns Where there was Once One: The Aldea in Medieval Aragon." *Mediterranean Studies* 6 (1996): 29–38.

———. "The Use and Misuse of 'Prohibited Arms' in Frontier Texas and Medieval Iberia." *Lamar Journal of the Humanities* 22 (1996): 5–18.

———. "Violence Management in Twelfth-Century Catalonia and Aragon." In *Marginated Groups in Spanish and Portuguese History*, ed. William D. Phillips, Jr. and Carla Rahn Phillips, 11–21. Minneapolis, 1989.

Kantorowicz, Ernst. *The King's Two Bodies: A Study in Medieval Political Theology.* Princeton, 1957; repr. Princeton, 1981.

Kempshall, M. S. *The Common Good in Late Medieval Political Thought.* Oxford, 1999.

Kennelly, Karen. "Catalan Peace and Truce Assemblies." *Studies in Medieval Culture* 5 (1975): 41–51.

———. "Sobre la paz de Dios y la sagrera en el condado de Barcelona (1030–1130)." *AEM* 5 (1968): 107–36.

King, P. D. *Law and Society in the Visigothic Kingdom.* Cambridge, 1972.

Kosto, Adam J. *Making Agreements in Medieval Catalonia: Power, Order, and the Written Word, 1000–1200.* Cambridge, 2000.

Lalinde Abadía, Jesús María. *Los fueros de Aragon.* Zaragoza, 1976.

———. *La jurisdicción real inferior en Cataluña ("Corts", "Veguers", "Batlles").* Madrid, 1966; repr. Barcelona, 1970.

———. *La persona y la obra del jurisconsulto vicense Jaume Callis.* Vich, 1980.

———. "Ordenamiento interno de la Corona de Aragón en la época de Jaime I." In X *CHCA*, Ponencias, 186–97.

Lea, Henry Charles. *The Duel and the Oath.* Parts I and II of idem, *Superstition and Force: Essays on the Wager of Battle, the Ordeal and Torture.* Philadelphia, 1866; repr. Philadelphia, 1974.

————. *The Ordeal*. Part III of *Superstition and Force*. Philadelphia, 1866; repr. Philadelphia, 1974.

Lewis, Archibald R. "Cataluña como frontera militar (870–1050)." *AEM* 5 (1968): 15–29.

————. *The Development of Southern French and Catalan Society, 718–1050*. Austin, TX, 1965.

Lladonosa Pujol, José. "Jaime I el conquistador y la ciudad de Lerida." In X *CHCA*, Comunicaciones, 1–2:449–60.

Lomax, Derek. *The Reconquest of Spain*. London, 1978.

Luscome, D. E. and G. R. Evans. "The Twelfth-Century Renaissance." In *Cambridge History of Medieval Political Thought*, 306–38.

Maddicott, J. R. *Simon de Montfort*. Cambridge, 1995.

Mann, Vivian, Thomas F. Glick, and Jerrilynn D. Dodds, eds. *Convivencia: Jews, Muslims, and Christians in Medieval Spain*. New York, 1992.

Maravall, José Antonio. *Estudios de historia del pensamiento español*. 2 vols, Madrid, 1972; repr. Madrid, 1983.

Martinez Ferrando, J. E. *La tràgica història dels reis de Mallorca*. Barcelona, 1975.

Marti, Ramon. "La integració a l'alou feudal de la seu de Girona de les terres beneficiades pel 'regim dels hispans': Els casos de Bàscara i Ullà, segles IX–XI." In *Formació*, 49–62.

Massip, J. "Els origans de l'administració de justicia a Tortosa des de la Carta de Població a les Costums." In X *CHCA*, Comunicaciones, 1–2:461–73.

Mateu i Lllopis Felipe. *Glosario hispánico de numismática*. Barcelona, 1940.

McCrank, Lawrence J. "Documenting Reconquest and Reform: The Growth of Archives in the Medieval Crown of Aragon." In *Medieval Frontier History in New Catalonia*, study 1, 305–18. Aldershot, 1996.

————. "Norman Crusaders in the Catalan Reconquest: Robert Burdet and the Principality of Tarragona, 1079–1155." In *Medieval Frontier History*, study IV, 67–82.

McKitterick, Rosamond. *The Carolingians and the Written Word*. Cambridge, 1989.

Miret i Sans, Joaquim. "Escolars catalans al estudi de Bolonia en la XIII al XIV centúria." *BRABLB* 8 (1915): 137–55.

————. *Itinerari de Jaume I "el Conqueridor."* Barcelona, 1918.

Mundó, Anscari M. "El Pacte de Cazola de 1179 i el 'Liber Feudorum Maior': Notas Paleogràfiques i Diplomàtiques." X *CHCA*, Comunicaciones, 1–2:119–29.

Myers, Henry A. *Medieval Kingship: The Origins and Development of Western Monarchy in All Stages From the Fall of Rome to the Fifteenth Century*. Chicago, 1972.

Nicholas, Karen S. "The Role of Feudal Relationships in the Consolidation of

Power in the Principalities of the Low Countries, 1000–1300." In *Law, Custom, and the Social Fabric*, 113–30.

Nörr, Knut Wolfgang. "Institutional Foundations of the New Jurisprudence." In *Renaissance and Renewal*, 324–38.

O'Callaghan, Joseph F. *A History of Medieval Spain*. Ithaca, NY, 1975.

———. "The Ideology of Government in the Reign of Alfonso X of Castile." *Exemplaria Hispanica* 1 (1991–1992): 1–17.

———. "Kings and Lords in Conflict in Late Thirteenth-Century Castile and Aragon." In *Iberia and the Mediterranean World*, 117–35.

———. *The Learned King. The Reign of Alfonso X of Castile*. Philadelphia, 1993.

Oman, Charles. *A History of the Art of War in the Middle Ages*. 2 vols. London, 1924.

Pennington, Kenneth. "Law, Legislative Authority and Theories of Government, 1150–1300." In *Cambridge History of Medieval Political Thought*, 424–53.

———. *The Prince and the Law, 1200–1600: Sovereignty and Rights in the Western Legal Tradition*. Berkeley, 1993.

Pererna i Espelt, Josep. "Les condiciones de la unió de Aragó i Catalunya en un manuscrit de Valencia: Rafael Marti de Viciana." *Arxiu de Textos Catalans Antics* 2 (1983): 357–61.

Pérez Bustamente, Lope Rogelio. "El gobierno y la administración de los territorios de la Corona de Aragón bajo Jaime I el Conquistador y su comparación con el regimen de Castilla y Navarra." In X *CHCA*, Comunicaciones, 1–2:515–32.

Perrin, John W. "Azo, Roman Law and Sovereign European States." *Studia Gratiana* 15 (1972): 92–101.

Plucknett, Theodore Frank Thomas. "The Relations between the Roman Law and the English Common Law down to the Sixteenth Century: A General Survey." *University of Toronto Journal* 3 (1939–1940): 24–50.

Pocock, J. G. A. *The Ancient Constitution and the Feudal Law: A Study of English Historical Thought in the Seventeenth Century*. Cambridge, 1957; repr. New York, 1967.

Poly, Jean-Pierre and Eric Bournazel. *The Feudal Transformation, 900–1200*, trans. Caroline Higgitt. New York, 1981.

Pons i Guri, Josep María. "Entre l'emfiteusi i el feudalisme (Els reculls de dret gironins)." In *Formació*, 411–18.

Portella i Comas, Jaume, ed. *La formació i expansió del feudalisme català*. Gerona, 1985–1986.

Post, Gaines. *Studies in Medieval Legal Thought, Public Law and the State, 1100–1321*. Princeton, 1968.

Procopé, Henry. "Greek and Roman Political Theory." In *Cambridge History of Medieval Political Thought,* 21–36.

Rashdall, Hastings. *The Universities of Europe in the Middle Ages,* ed. F. M. Powicke and A. B. Emden. 3 vols. Oxford, 1935; repr. Oxford, 1997.

Read, Jan. *The Catalans.* London, 1978.

Reilly. Bernard F. *The Medieval Spains.* Cambridge, 1993.

Reynolds, Susan. *Fiefs and Vassals: The Medieval Evidence Reinterpreted.* Oxford, 1994.

Riché, Pierre. *Daily Life in the World of Charlemagne,* trans. Jo Ann McNamara. Philadelphia, 1973; repr. Philadelphia, 1983.

Rodón Binué, Eulalia. *El lenguaje técnico del feudalismo en el siglo XI en Cataluña. Contribución al estudio de latin medieval.* Barcelona, 1957.

Rubió i Lluch, Antonio. *Documents per l'història de la cultura catalana mig-eval.* 2 vols. Barcelona, 1908–1921.

Sanpere y Miquel, Salvador. "Minoría de Jaime I." In I *CHCA,* 2:581–694.

Santamaría, Alvaro. "La expansión politico-militar de la Corona de Aragón: Baleares." In X *CHCA,* Ponencias, 91–109.

Sarasa Sánchez, Esteban. *Aragón y el compromiso de Caspe.* Zaragoza, 1981.

———. *Sociedad y conflictos sociales en Aragón s. XIII–XV (Estructuras de poder y conflictos de clase).* Madrid, 1981.

Sitges, J. B. *La muerte de D. Bernardo de Cabrera, consejero del rey d. Pedro IV de Aragón.* Madrid, 1911.

Smith, Cyril E. *The University of Toulouse in the Middle Ages.* Milwaukee, WI, 1958.

Sobrequès i Vidal, Santiago. *Els barons de Catalunya.* Barcelona, 1957; repr. Barcelona, 1980.

———. *Els primers comtes catalans.* Barcelona, 1957; repr. Barcelona, 1983.

Soldevila, Ferran. *Història de Catalunya.* 3 vols. Barcelona, 1934; repr. Barcelona, 1962.

———. *Pere el Gran.* 4 vols. Barcelona, 1950-1962.

———. *Els primers temps de Jaume I.* Barcelona, 1968.

———. "A propòsit del servei del bovatge." *AEM* 1 (1954): 753–87.

Sorío, F. Balthasar. *De viris illustribus Provinciae Aragoniae Ordinis Predicatorum.* Valencia, 1950.

Strayer, Joseph R. *The Albigensian Crusades.* Ann Arbor, MI, 1994.

———. "Feudalism." In *DMA,* 5:52–57.

———. "Feudalism in Western Europe." In *Feudalism in History,* ed. Rushton Coulborn, 15–24. Hamden, CT, 1965.

————. *On the Medieval Origins of the Modern State*. Princeton, 1970.

Structures féodales et féodalisme dans l'Occident méditerranéen, X^e–XIIIe siècles: bilan et perspectives de recherche. Colloque international organisé par le Recherche Scientifique et l'École Française de Rome, Rome, 10–13 October 1978. Rome, 1983.

Tierney, Brian. *The Idea of Natural Rights: Studies on Natural Rights, Natural Law, and Church Law, 1150–1625*. Atlanta, GA, 1996.

Traggia, Joaquím. "Illustración del reynado de don Ramiro de Aragón." *MRAH* 3 (1799): 497–592.

Trenchs Odena, Josep. "La escribanía de Ramón Berenguer III (1097–1131): Datos biográficos." *Saitabi* 31 (1984): 11–36.

Truax, Jean A. "Anglo-Norman Women at War: Valiant Soldiers, Prudent Strategists or Charismatic Leaders?" In *The Circle of War in the Middle Ages: Essays on Medieval Military and Naval History*, ed. Donald J. Kagay and L. J. Andrew Villalon, 111–25. Woodbridge, Suffolk, 1999.

Ubieto Arteta, Antonio "La reconquista de Valencia y Murcia." In X *CHCA*, Ponencias, 147–66.

Ullmann, Walter. *The Individual and Society in the Middle Ages*. Baltimore, 1966.

————. *Law and Politics in the Middle Ages: An Introduction to the Sources of Medieval Political Ideas*. Ithaca, NY, 1975.

————. *The Medieval Idea of Law as Represented by Lucas of Penna*. New York, 1969.

Valdeavellano y Arcimus, Luis García de. *Curso de historia de las instituciones españoles de los orígenes al final de la edad media*. Madrid, 1968.

Valls Taberner, Ferran. "Los abogados en Cataluña durante la edad media." In idem, *Obras selectas*, 4 vols. 2:281–318. Madrid, 1954–1961.

————. "Un articulat inédit de *Consuetuds de Barcelona*." In idem, *Obras* 2:142–47.

————. "Les doctrines politiques de la Catalunya medieval." In idem, *Obras* 2:210–16.

————. "Notes sobre el duel judicial." In idem, *Obras* 2:247–57.

————. "Ordinacions navals catalanes del segle XIV." In idem, *Obras* 2:198–200.

van den Bergh, G. C. J. J. "The Concept of Folk Law in Historical Context: A Brief Outline." In *Folk Law: Essays in the Theory and Practice of 'Lex Non Scripta',*" ed. Alison Dundes Renteln and Alan Dundes, 2 vols. 1:5–31. Madison, WI, 1994.

van Caenegem, R. C. "Galbert of Bruges." In *Law, Custom and the Social Fabric*, 89–112.

————. "Law and Power in Twelfth-Century Flanders." In *Cultures of Power*, 149–71.

———. "Government, Law and Society." In *Cambridge History of Medieval Political Thought*, 174–210.

Van Kleffens, E. N. *Hispanic Law until the End of the Middle Ages*. Edinburgh, 1968.

Vann, Theresa M. "The Town Council of Toledo during the Minority of Alfonso VIII (1158–1169)." In *Medieval Iberia: Essays on the History and Literature of Medieval Spain*, ed. Donald J. Kagay and Joseph T. Snow, 43–60. New York, 1997.

Verrié, F.-P. "La política artística de Pere el Ceremoniós." In *Pere el Ceremoniós*. 177–92.

Vinagradoff, Paul. *Roman Law in Medieval Europe*. Oxford, 1929.

Vicens Vives, Jaume. *Història de las remensas (en el sigle XV)*. Barcelona, 1976.

Wasserstein, David. *The Rise and Fall of the Party-Kings*. Princeton, 1985.

Watson, Alan. *The Evolution of Law*. Baltimore, 1985.

Wolf, Armin. "Die Gesetzgebung der entstehenden Territorialstaaten." In *Handbuch der Quellen und Literatur der neueren europäischen Privatrechts geschichte*, ed. Helmut Coing, 3 vols. 1:517–800. Munich, 1973–1988.

Wolff, Hans Julius. *Roman Law. An Historical Introduction*. Norman, OK, 1951; repr. Norman, OK, 1976.

Zacour, Norman. *An Introduction to Medieval Institutions*. New York, 1976.

Zurita y Castro, Jeronimo. *Anales de la Corona de Aragón*, ed. Angel Canellas López, 9 vols. Zaragoza, 1967–1985.

Counties of Catalonia

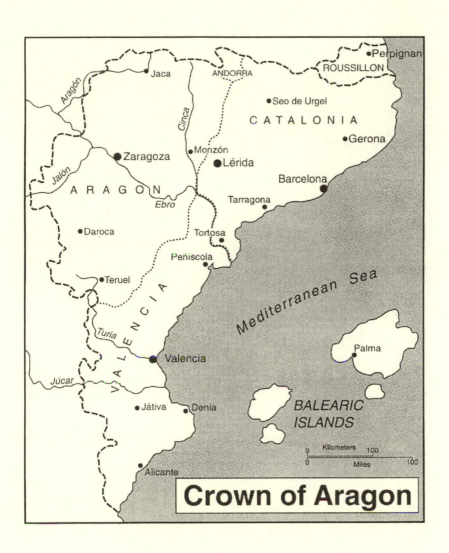

Crown of Aragon

Map labels: Perpignan, ROUSSILLON, Jaca, ANDORRA, Seo de Urgel, CATALONIA, Aragón, Cinca, Monzón, Zaragoza, Lérida, Gerona, Jalón, ARAGON, Barcelona, Ebro, Tarragona, Daroca, Tortosa, Peñiscola, Teruel, VALENCIA, Mediterranean Sea, Turia, Palma, Valencia, Júcar, Játiva, Denia, BALEARIC ISLANDS, Alicante

Kilometers 0 100
Miles 0 100

Barcelona Dynasty

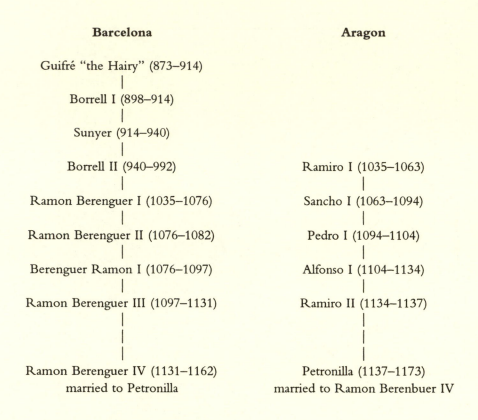

Barcelona	Aragon

Guifré "the Hairy" (873–914)
|
Borrell I (898–914)
|
Sunyer (914–940)
|
Borrell II (940–992)　　　　　Ramiro I (1035–1063)
|　　　　　　　　　　　　　　　|
Ramon Berenguer I (1035–1076)　　Sancho I (1063–1094)
|　　　　　　　　　　　　　　　|
Ramon Berenguer II (1076–1082)　　Pedro I (1094–1104)
|　　　　　　　　　　　　　　　|
Berenguer Ramon I (1076–1097)　　Alfonso I (1104–1134)
|　　　　　　　　　　　　　　　|
Ramon Berenguer III (1097–1131)　　Ramiro II (1134–1137)
|　　　　　　　　　　　　　　　|
|　　　　　　　　　　　　　　　|
|　　　　　　　　　　　　　　　|
Ramon Berenguer IV (1131–1162)　　Petronilla (1137–1173)
married to Petronilla　　　　married to Ramon Berenbuer IV

Crown of Aragon

Alfonso II {Alfons I} (1163–1196)
|
Pedro II {Pere I} (1196–1213)
|
Jaime I {Jaume I} (1213–1276)
|
Pedro III {Pere II} (1276–1285)
|
Alfonso III {Alfons II} (1285–1291)
|
Jaime II {Jaume II} (1291–1327)
|
Alfonso IV {Alfons III} (1327–1336)
|
Pedro IV {Pere III} (1336–1387)
|
Juan I {Joan I} (1387–1396)
|
Martin I {Martí I} (1396–1410)

Interregnum (1410–1412)

Trastámara Dynasty

Fernando I {Ferran I} (1412–1416)
|
Alfonso V {Alfons IV} (1416–1458)
|
Juan II {Joan II} (1458–1479)
|
Fenando II {Ferran II} (1479–1516)

One of the bitterest disputes of twentieth-century medieval scholarship of America and Europe has centered on the nature of feudalism, one school denying its existence while the other espoused the traditional view that feudal relations comprised the baserock of medieval society. A middle road is possible with the investigation of the legal guidebooks that began to appear throughout Europe in the early thirteenth century. One of the most interesting but least known of these works, *The Customs of Catalonia*, is a legal treatise on feudal relations and castle tenure written in the mid-thirteenth century by the Barcelona canon and royal attorney, Pere Albert. From the study of such practical handbooks, social and political historians of the Middle Ages may gain a more nuanced view of the legal relations of lord and vassals in Catalonia, one of the most "feudalized" areas of early medieval Europe. Donald J. Kagay has made this material accessible to students and specialists alike with an English translation and introductions that place Pete Albert's in the context of the thirteenth-century legal handbooks of France and England as well as in the "feudalism debate" of the twentieth century.

Donald J. Kagay is an associate professor at Albany State University (Georgia).